Helping Children
Survive Divorce

Helping Children Survive Divorce

What to Expect; How to Help

Formerly *Children & Divorce—*
Revised and updated

by

Dr. Archibald D. Hart

WORD PUBLISHING
Dallas•London•Vancouver•Melbourne

Library of Congress Cataloging-in-Publication Data

Hart, Archibald D.
  Helping children survive divorce : what to expect, how to help / by
Archibald D. Hart.
    p. cm.
  Rev. and updated ed. of : Children & divorce. 1989.
  ISBN 0–8499–3949–6
  1. Children of divorced parents. 2. Divorced parents. I. Hart,
Archibald D. Children & divorce. II. Title.
HQ777.5.H37 1997
306.89—dc21
                                                            96–51885
                                                            CIP

Printed in the United States of America
89012349 QKP 987654

To
Gertrude and Henry—

I will always be thankful
for the life you gave me.

Contents

Acknowledgments

There have been many over the years who have prepared me for this book. My grandparents, long since deceased, were the most helpful healing source in my life. They taught me faith in God and pointed me in the right direction in life. I will always be thankful for grandparents.

My wonderful wife, Kathleen, has also been a constant inspiration to me. As the most transparent, genuine, and vibrant person I have ever known, she has helped my healing immensely over the forty-two years of our marriage.

My three daughters, Catherine, Sharon, and Sylvia, cannot be left out of any credit for my healing either. Children have a way of bringing up parents and imparting wholeness simply from their presence in your world. Thank you for being so tolerant and loving despite the many mistakes I have made as a father.

To my many patients who have contributed to my clinical experience and who have taught me more than any textbook, I also want to express my deepest gratitude. You will search in vain for your own stories here as I have disguised the details and changed the circumstances cited to protect your confidentiality. However, you need to take credit for the principles I set out and for the help this book provides others.

Finally, my secretary, Linda Rojas, has patiently carried me through my sabbatical year, providing support and continuity despite my extensive travel and speaking engagements. She did the final reading of the manuscript and helped me enormously with many tasks.

Archibald D. Hart

Preface

Are the children of divorce any different from other children? On the outside they don't appear to be. They laugh, cry, wear the latest fads, and watch the same television shows as other children. But are they different? I believe they are, and I am speaking from personal experience as well as from professional knowledge.

My parents divorced when I was twelve years of age. That singular event changed my life forever. As a psychotherapist I have also worked with many divorcing and divorced families over the years. My wife and I have also taught many seminars to clergy, couples, and divorced groups. This experience has convinced me that the children of the average, hostile dissolution of marriage are indeed influenced by the process, and they are likely to be different from other children as a consequence.

Why is this so? Simply because divorce, while no longer the stigma it once was, is not a small thing in a child's experience. It sets up a wrenching, painful, tragic series of events that forces a series of adjustments and changes that the children are not always capable of making. These adjustments *always* leave their mark; it is just a matter of *how big a mark* remains when all the dust settles. And then the real trouble begins. Most postdivorce periods are acrimonious and often do more damage than the divorce itself, often leaving permanent emotional scars on all the parties, but especially the children.

I have seen and felt enough to convince me that divorce is not the neutral, the-child-will-get-over-it-quickly life-event that many would have us believe. It is a serious and complex cause of mental health problems today. It is a crisis of immense proportions facing children all over the world.

I want to say to the reader that most research in this area backs up what I have to say in this book, namely that the effects of divorce on children are far reaching, more serious and long-lasting than most divorce advocates are willing to admit. There are a few researchers who believe otherwise, and I will try to be fair and give their conclusions also.

In case this sounds too gloomy and negative, let me hasten to add the good news. The children of divorce are not always irrevocably damaged or emotionally tarnished. Everything depends on how the divorcing parents behave and how they help their children adjust to the marriage dissolution. It is possible that, with the right guidance, parents can help their children to become better-adjusted, healthier, and more successful than otherwise, but it will take some work. And that is what this book is all about.

Are the children of Christian parents any better off in a divorce? I believe not. If anything, I would venture to suggest that in many instances they are in a worse situation. Why? In addition to the problems that any child has to face in adjusting to the breakup of the home, the child of Christian parents has to confront the failure of their religious system to resolve the conflict in the home. The child has to struggle with such questions as: "Why didn't God make Mommy and Daddy love each other?" "Why doesn't God answer my prayers?" And for the older child an even more devastating thought: "Does Christianity really work?" The child could easily become disillusioned with Christianity and come to seriously question whether spiritual values are helpful or important.

The purpose of this book, then, is to provide help for divorcing parents as well as for other concerned adults in the child's life. Grandparents, as we will see, can do much to minimize the long-term damages of divorce. So, also, can relatives, friends, and even schoolteachers.

Realistically, my goal here is to show parents how to *minimize* the damaging effects of divorce and to turn whatever havoc that cannot be avoided into an influence for good. We cannot eliminate all pain. Not only is this unrealistic, it isn't helpful. Some emotional pain is necessary for character formation. Trees that grow tall without wind fall over easily. It takes the pressure of the wind to force roots to grow strong. Hopefully, parents can turn their disaster into a strong wind of growth.

This book is written from a Christian perspective, and for this I make no apologies. I am of the opinion that the children of Christian parents are at greater risk than others. However, I certainly hope that no matter what your religious affiliation, if any, this book will help you to build a healthier postdivorce life for your children. Perhaps they can be counted among the few who not only survived divorce but became the better for it. I certainly count myself among this fortunate group.

CHAPTER 1

Divorced at Twelve

My mother kept telling me, "It's not the end of the world." But how do you convince a child of twelve that the breakup of his family is not the end of everything secure and stable?

My mother was packing our suitcases. My brother, only ten years of age, seemed less bothered than I. He had already developed a reputation for being tough. He never cried, no matter how badly he'd been hurt. My parents could spank him and he would never flinch. The sight of suitcases spread around my mother's bedroom even excited him, as if it meant we were going on some holiday adventure.

In typical older-brother fashion I said to myself, "He's too young to understand what is happening. I'll have to handle this for both of us."

I was frantic. How could my mother be doing this to us? Had she gone crazy? I knew that she had been unhappy for a long time, but how was running away going to solve anything? I tried pleading with her. Would she reconsider her actions? Couldn't she see I was frightened? She replied that I didn't understand these matters, that I was too young to know about adult things.

The pain in my chest got worse. My head felt dizzy, as if it were going to explode. I was running out of ideas for making her see reason.

Feelings kept flip-flopping. One moment I felt old for my years, as if

I were being called upon to carry a burden that was too heavy for me. Then I felt childish and helpless again. I started to cry, softly at first, and then my sobs became angry screams directed at my mother. I told her that I hated her, but she only ignored me. She knew how to handle hysterical people.

Softly she told me to hurry up with my packing. "Make sure you take everything you need for school. I don't intend to come back here to fetch anything you forget." I knew she meant business, so reluctantly I complied, even though I felt that this was the end of the world for me.

I can't remember much of what happened after that. I know my throbbing heart ached as if I were having a heart attack. I believe I became quiet and withdrew to another room as I realized how pointless my resistance was.

I sat there brooding. My mother had not directly come out and said, "I'm going to divorce your father." She merely presented it as wanting to live away from him. Either she wasn't very clear in her own mind about what she wanted to do, or she was protecting me from further hurt by taking the divorce in stages. But I knew what was happening, and the fact that she was not being honest with me only made it worse. In retrospect, it was knowing so little that fed my anxiety. If I had known more, I believe I would have dealt with the calamity better.

Why Did Mother Want a Divorce?

My reason for telling the story of my childhood divorce is to help divorcing parents get a better feel for what their children go through. Having heard many other personal stories, I can say mine is no different from most.

My mother and father had been fighting for years. Even now, as I reflect on their marriage, I don't fully understand why it was so conflicted. Partly, I believe, it was that they had married so young, before their adult personalities had fully formed. It was the early thirties, the Great Depression had hit South Africa as well as the rest of the Western world. Work was scarce, so my father had decided to move to the gold-mining area where prospects were greater. He married his girlfriend so as not to complicate matters by being three hundred miles apart. Clearly, they married too young, and they plainly outgrew each other as they matured.

But that wasn't the whole story. Their problems also stemmed from their inability to communicate clearly with each other. Of course, one must bear in mind that not a lot was known about marital communication in those days before the war. You wonder how anyone made marriage work, let alone prosper. Yet my grandparents evidenced a happy marriage. They could talk through their conflicts, even big ones. But my parents could not resolve even relatively minor issues to the point of understanding and agreement.

They were both very insecure. I think many young people of that era were. Life, when surrounded by severe economic depression, can have a way of unsettling you. Their mutual insecurity made them extremely jealous of each other. As a result they each became very possessive and controlling, especially my father. There was no freedom in their relationship and little happiness in their intimacy.

One question often haunts me. Would their marriage have survived if they had been Christians—I mean real Christians? They were nominal church attenders. They saw to it that my brother and I went to Sunday school regularly, and for this I am eternally grateful. I don't recall any period of my childhood, until I was seventeen, when I was not attending church. They advocated honesty and valued sincerity. But they knew nothing of a God who could take control of their hurts and help them give and receive forgiveness. They knew nothing about prayer and could not have found any word of promise or encouragement from Scripture even if they had wanted to. Could they have survived if they had known how to use these resources? I like to believe they could have!

The Emotional Aftereffects

In the months after we left the house, we lived first in a hotel and then in an apartment. My father was grief-stricken by the separation and went into an angry depression. He tried everything to make amends to my mother, but she would not give in. Finally, she filed for divorce and the die was cast for our changed lives.

But what were the emotional aftereffects of the divorce? During this time I was extremely unhappy. I couldn't sleep. I lost interest in my many hobbies. I didn't want to go to school because I became pessimistic about the future. I understand this pessimism a little now as I try to help my twelve-year-old grandson adjust to the loss of his father who was tragically killed in an automobile accident nine months ago. My grandson sees no point in going to school. Life is over as far as he is concerned. That is exactly how I felt.

Nothing seemed to matter anymore to me. I went from being a conscientious kid to being a problem. I began to do things that bothered my parents, such as not bothering to tie my shoelaces. I suspect that this was partly a way of getting attention from my mother; untied shoelaces make a clickity-click sound as you slop around, and sooner or later someone notices. But partly it was that I didn't care about life anymore.

My irritating behavior took other forms as well. My socks began appearing in unmatched pairs, and no matter how I tried, I was late for everything—meals, school, and music lessons.

In retrospect I can see that much of my behavior was an attempt to punish my parents for their actions. If they could see how troubled I was, I must have thought to myself, though I have no recollection of it, perhaps they would come together again and we could all live happily ever after—the stuff that fairy tales are made of. It didn't happen, of course. By and large my behaviors were ignored. My mother was too preoccupied with her own emotional pain and had little energy left to deal with mine. That was both good and bad. She didn't reinforce my bad behavior, but on the other hand I had no healthy way to express what I was feeling.

Gradually I gave up on the manipulative maneuvers and gave in to a genuine feeling of grief. I was in mourning just as if someone I loved had died; the full reality of the divorce had finally hit home. The pain, which to this point had seemed to be in my chest, now settled in my stomach. I now know this to be a sign of a shift from fear and anxiety (pain in the chest) to depression (pain in the stomach). I didn't understand it, but the process of healing had begun. A pain in the stomach is a good sign!

I can't recall how long my grieving lasted. I suppose the intense part was over in three or four weeks, but this was followed by a low-level depression that must have lasted for a long time—possibly many years. Actually, the grieving process came in spasms. First there was the major grief reaction over the loss of the family unit, but this was followed by a series of awarenesses of the other losses that go with being divorced. Some of these I became aware of only in the months and years that followed. To help parents understand what a child goes through in divorce, let me list just a few of the losses I experienced:

+ Loss of my home
+ Loss of my neighborhood friends
+ Loss of convenient transportation (We only had one automobile in the family.)
+ Dramatic reduction in our standard of living
+ Loss of family outings together

These were all tangible losses to me. There were many others that were too abstract for me to identify, but they contributed their share to the pain I felt also.

One of the painful necessities I had to face during this time was telling my friends about the divorce. Divorce, while becoming more common, still had a stigma attached to it, and the children of our neighborhood tended to react not so much out of pity for me, but out of fear that something like this could happen to them. The reaction of my friends was far from sympathetic. They seemed to panic as much as I did.

At night, while I was trying to go to sleep, my imagination would have a field day; my mind would feed me all sorts of ridiculous ideas. I would fantasize, for instance, that somehow my parents would get back together, and I would picture our united family smiling together. But most of my fantasies were negative. I would imagine I was grown up and looking for employment. In the job interview I would be asked, "Are you a divorced child?" I would have to reply, "Yes, I am," and would then be told, "I'm sorry, but we don't have a position for you." It seems crazy now, but that's what a mind does when it is in turmoil.

My worst fantasy was that I would never have a girlfriend. One of my friends told me that people from divorced homes never stay married. So what would the parents of girls think of me if my parents were divorced?

I was just beginning to see girls as necessary and desirable and not as nuisances. One girl in my school had attracted my attention. She seemed friendly toward me and invited me to her home to meet her parents. The night before I worried about what they would think if they knew I was a divorced child? Could I keep it a secret from them? What would happen if they eventually found out? I withdrew from her friendship to avoid embarrassment and hurt and even considered living the rest of my life as a hermit, or whatever it was that meant you never got married!

While I didn't quite become a recluse, I did shun social contacts for a while. I became very self-conscious, convinced that everybody was looking at me and talking about me and my family behind my back. I feared that they were shunning me as if I were diseased. I can clearly remember listening with rapt attention in Sunday school to the story of Jesus healing the leper. I knew exactly what it felt like to be an outcast and needing to warn everyone when you approached so they would not be contaminated by your disease. I felt like a divorce leper!

Feelings for Mother

When my mother first took us away from our home, I directed all my anger at her. She was, after all, the one who initiated the family breakup. In my rage, I wanted to humiliate her, even physically hurt her.

It is very hard for a child with such feelings to think clearly. I was oblivious to my mother's pain; I thought only of myself and how her actions were going to affect me. This is, after all, the natural self-preservation instinct God has built into each of us.

The security of a family and the assurance of stability are essential for healthy development in all of us, so I am no different in this respect. We instinctively need a haven where we can take refuge from the storms of growing up, a harbor in which we can build a vessel strong enough to brave the storms of a cruel and unstable world. When this security is threatened, every protective instinct God has created in us is mobilized. It is no wonder, therefore, that divorce makes a child so angry! It threatens the very foundation of his or her existence.

When the separation between my parents was formally established and my brother and I began to visit our father, my anger toward my mother turned to feelings of hatred. I became disrespectful, trying to make sure she knew how much she had hurt me and how she was destroying our lives. Sometimes I refused to speak to her, using silence as a weapon. She was entirely to blame, I felt, not just for the misery in the marriage (I was fully aware of my father's contribution to this), but for initiating the breakup.

But the worst was yet to come. Shortly after the divorce was finalized, my mother announced that she was getting married again. I now felt that my destruction was complete. This was the absolute end. Nothing could be worse than this. The fantasies of reconciliation were shattered. My conscious wish and prayer that somehow God was going to pull off a miracle and unite us all again vanished into thin air. Once again feelings of despair and hopelessness set in, only much more intense.

I had known nothing of my mother's dating. She had started seeing another man shortly after the separation and had somehow been able to keep it a secret. It turned out that this man was to be a significant person in my healing, but I was not to know this at this stage. I demanded that I be allowed to live with my father.

Feelings for Father

Through the early years of my childhood I had developed a love-hate relationship with my father. I admired many of his skills; I believed he could build anything, repair anything, do anything. And many of his skills have rubbed off on me. He was fun to play with. His stories about his childhood and teenage exploits enthralled my brother and me. It appeared to us that he was the local daredevil who led many of his friends into petty pranks and exciting exploits. I would rather have heard him tell of his midnight pranks than watch a modern Batman movie. His stories were so much more exciting.

But I was also aware that he was a jealous and possessive person. He became angry easily. Life at home was far from pleasant for all of us, but as children we had adjusted to it. We knew when to shut up, and we knew when to keep out of the way of marital squabbles. Despite this trouble at home I had never suspected that the marriage was on the verge of breaking up. I thought that we would always be this way.

With the first blow of the separation, my love-hate feelings for my father turned to pity. I really felt sorry for him, even though deep down I knew he had brought this pain on himself. When my brother and I visited him, he would probe us about what was happening. Questions like "Has your mother changed her mind?" or "When are you coming back?" were constantly fired at us. Soon I began to feel apprehensive whenever I visited him. I didn't like what was going on between all of us.

Slowly my feelings of pity turned to feelings of anger and resentment. He wanted my brother and me to stay with him. I suspected that this was his way of manipulating my mother, so I resisted at first. While I blamed her for initiating the divorce, I also knew she was only reacting to a painful situation. I knew how insecure she felt and how much she needed us to help her feel safe and not abandoned. Slowly I became aware of how my father was using us as pawns, quite unconsciously I am sure. He would not deliberately have hurt us, but he was desperate; he felt his very survival was being threatened.

Feelings for God

My grandmother was a very devout Christian. During my early childhood her influence on me was profound. God was real to her, and somehow that was all the proof for the existence of God that I needed at that young age. She would read Scripture to us, pray, and sing hymns with us. And it was always happy singing; her faith was a joyful faith.

My grandparents lived about 120 miles from our hometown in a small rural, community. Their town is situated on the banks of a large river which attracts a lot of holiday camping activity. Large numbers of city people would go there during the holiday season to camp, swim, sunbathe, boat, and explore the many islands of the wide African river. My grandparents had moved there after my grandfather retired, and they were able to live off the small farm they had established.

My brother and I spent every school holiday with my grandparents, partly because it was fun, but partly to get away from the tension at home. We loved being on that farm! I dreaded returning home after a stay with my grandparents, because I was never sure what I could expect. Would my parents be on speaking terms or not? Would there be discord or not? Sometimes a return home would be happy. Most times it was miserable.

And so I learned to pray. Four or five days before we were due to go home after a stay with my grandparents, I would pray frequently. My prayer was simple: "Please God, make Mommy and Daddy happy." Sometimes it worked. Mostly it didn't. I considered talking to my grandmother about why prayer is sometimes answered and sometimes not, but I didn't want her to know how bad things were at home. So I said nothing.

Slowly my prayers changed from simple requests to outright demands. "God, you've got to make Mommy and Daddy happy." Then they became angry prayers. I argued with God. I threatened him. "Why don't you make them happy? What's wrong with you? Don't you love me? Don't you care?"

At about the time my mother told us she was separating from my father, I began to think that God was using my parents' fighting to punish me. The reason he wasn't answering my prayer was that I had been naughty, so I tried to find ways to atone for my sin so that God didn't have to punish me. Everything I did or thought was carefully scrutinized to see whether I was displeasing God.

After the separation, I slowly came to realize that nothing was going to change. My mother was determined to get her freedom and start a new life. So a feeling of helplessness set in as I realized there was nothing I could do to change the situation or influence the outcome of the divorce. This resulted in a hopeless feeling, and I distinctly remember coming to the conclusion that the reason God wasn't answering my prayers was that God didn't exist. Or if he did he was too busy with other worlds or other parts of my world to care about me.

The Healing of My Emotions

It would be very sad if my experience with God had ended at this point. To be disillusioned with parents is bad enough; to feel abandoned by

God is devastating. But that wasn't the end! I was too caught up in my pain to know it, but the slow process of healing was taking place even when I felt things were at their worst—and God was clearly a part of that healing.

I floundered in my emotional turmoil for about a year after my parents' divorce was finalized. Part of my distress was a consequence of the depression I felt in response to the loss of our family unit, but the subsequent disorganization of our family life also contributed to the problem.

When my mother announced her intention to remarry, my brother and I decided we would live with our father, at least for a while. This upset my mother, but she conceded to our request. I think she was too exhausted to put up any fight.

In the year following the divorce my father moved us at least four times, searching for a living situation that was satisfactory. Everything seemed to go wrong, and my father was too angry and upset to help us much. I had to start a new high school and make new friends. It wasn't easy when you didn't have a stable home life!

It was about this time that healing really began for me. (In retrospect, I marvel at the resilience of the human spirit; it takes a great deal of punishment to make any permanent dent in its armor.) There were three sources of help for my healing: my grandparents, my Sunday school teacher, and, believe it or not, my mother's new husband.

My grandparents were extremely loving and supportive toward my brother and me during this period. If they were angry at my parents, they never showed or talked about it to us. They never interfered, except to invite us to visit them as often as we wanted. We slipped in a few weekend visits that were not a part of our regular visiting schedule, and those visits were like an oasis in a dry desert. They provided relief from the tensions at home and helped me to keep my perspective and sanity. There was always the reassurance that if things really got bad I could go and live with my grandparents; they had said as much. I even sneaked out one day while staying with them to check out the local high school. It was comforting to know that there was an alternative. Having an anxious disposition, I needed this assurance.

All through my childhood years and until I was seventeen I had attended the Sunday school of our local church. While on the outside I would play the tough guy with all my high-school friends (many didn't seem to go to church at all) and made out that I was only going to church because my parents forced me to, deep down I found church very satisfying.

One Sunday school teacher in particular impressed me greatly. She was the mother of another boy my age and also served as the superintendent of our Sunday school. In her youth she had contracted polio, so she walked with a limp. But what really impressed me was her ability to give unconditional love. She exuded it. She looked you in the eyes and her expression seemed to shout, "I love you just the way you are!" She never became irritated or angry at us, no matter what we did. She was a beautiful person through and through.

She obviously knew about the breakup of our home, although she never embarrassed me over it or made it a big issue. But I could feel her love and concern; it was in her eyes and in the way she touched me— gentle but firm. Her unspoken message was very clear: "There is more to life than raiment, and more to live for than parents." And I started to believe her!

Through this woman's influence, Matthew 6:33 became an important verse of Scripture to me: "Seek ye first the kingdom of God, and his righteousness; and all these things shall be added unto you." I came to know God personally, not for what he could do in saving our family, but for what he had done for me in dying on the cross. These words helped to free me from bitterness and hatred and moved me to the place of forgiveness for all the deep hurts and resentment I had experienced. They helped me overcome the aftereffects of losing the most precious thing a child can have—his family. (When my wife and I became engaged years later, I had Matthew 6:33 inscribed on the inside of her engagement ring. It is still there, forty-two years later!)

When my mother remarried, I was too numb to feel anything. It seemed I had felt it all already. What more was there to experience? I did not meet my new stepfather until after the wedding, because my brother and I had already moved in with my father, and it didn't seem appropriate that I should have contact with him.

In the months that followed the wedding I occasionally encountered him, although I kept my distance. But this man simply accepted me for what I was and showered me with kindness. Although I was just thirteen years old, he treated me as an adult, showing respect for my opinions and even asking me to express them. He never put me down and never once insinuated that I was an intruder when I visited my mother. Slowly I came to trust him, and slowly my fears subsided. Imperceptibly, but very definitely, I began to see life return to normal again. New patterns emerged. Change was not an impossible mountain to climb.

My brother and I finally moved back to live with my mother when my father remarried and moved across the country. His life was also recovering, and my new stepmother turned out to be a real gem of a person. My mother had two more sons, and both became a part of my life, though we are separated by vast oceans.

I am now getting on in years, reasonably successful and extremely happy—and I mean extremely. My marriage of more than forty years is the pride of my life; my wife, whom I cherish very deeply, is a wonderful provision from God. My three daughters are the best a father could hope for. And what can I possibly say to impress you about the most wonderful seven grandchildren anyone could have?

But I often ask myself whether my life would have been easier and even happier in its earlier years if my parents had worked out their problems and stayed together. Even though my mother and father built separate but happy lives for themselves before they passed away I will always suspect that what emerged was only second best.

I thank God for second chances. Where would we be without them? So don't misunderstand me here. All I am saying is that we must make the most of our first chances. Or, if we now have a second chance, let's make the most of it. And whatever else happens, let us see to it that we give first priority to ensuring that our children, who are the least equipped to deal with our mistakes, don't reap the fruit of our sins.

CHAPTER 2

The Damaging Effects of Divorce

Debbie was always a cheerful and outgoing person. Despite the fact that she was slightly underdeveloped for her age, she never brooded about it and could even laugh at the jokes her schoolmates would make about her training bra. But then one day she lost her cool. "Get away from me—I hate you!" was all she would say to her friends. She would slip out of class before anyone could stop her for conversation. She became withdrawn and sullen.

"Is something bothering you, Debbie?" her schoolteacher asked her one day.

"Nothing's bothering me—I'm just sick of the world," was her reply.

Danny was quite the opposite—quiet and soft-spoken. As a high-school senior his gentleness made him popular with the girls, and while he didn't have a lot of self-confidence, he was successful at most of the activities he engaged in. He seemed to be set for a generous scholarship at a good college with the prospect of fulfilling a longtime dream of becoming a physician.

One day he arrived at school to take a biology test. He sat down at his desk, pulled out a pencil from inside his coat pocket, and twirled it between his fingers. The other kids worked energetically at the test, choosing the correct answers from the multiple options given; erasing the incorrect ones. Danny just sat there, twirling his pencil.

The teacher noticed this and asked him, "Is something bothering you, Danny?"

Danny stood up from his desk and without a word of explanation walked out of the room. Two months later he was arrested for being drunk and disorderly.

These stories, and many like them, can be told all across the country. What do they have in common? They are stories about the children of divorce. Like myself these children have gone through one of life's most wrenching and painful experiences—the disintegration of their homes.

One of the detrimental effects of my childhood experience of divorce was on my attitude toward crying. I hated myself when I cried. I deplored people who cried. My disgust with crying stemmed from my determined effort as a child not to show any pain, no matter how bad. Why did I do this? I suppose it was because I feared my father would make fun of me. He didn't respect people who cried. He never did and even boasted about how "tough" he was as a kid.

So, imagine my surprise when I began training for my second career as a psychologist and psychotherapist (for the first fifteen years of my adulthood I was a civil engineer). Very early I was confronted by a major obstacle—people in pain cried a lot and it made me very uncomfortable. I decided, therefore, that I would force myself to tolerate crying. After all, patients in turmoil are bound to want to cry a lot in a therapist's office. You see it in the movies all the time!

So I learned how to put up with other people's tears, and even, over time, became quite empathetic with their pain. But I kept a very strict supremacy over my own tears. Other people could, and should, cry. It was good for them. For me, tears were taboo—a sign of weakness that had to be kept under control.

It wasn't until about ten years into my new profession that I really came to terms with my own avoidance of crying—and learned of its healing power firsthand. Now I cry freely and unashamedly, as anyone who has ever been in one of my seminars knows.

In retrospect, I can see that my freedom to cry came only after my mother's death. Who knows, perhaps I had perpetuated a deep feeling of resentment toward her ever since she decided to divorce my father!

Whatever the reason, after her death a new openness developed toward my need to cry. Now I can cry freely when I need to and feel the freedom of this healthy emotional outlet. But it has taken a long time to undo this damaging consequence of my parents' divorce, coming as it did at such a critical stage of my life's development.

The Damaging Consequences of Divorce

Someone has described divorce as "the forever funeral." I can think of no more accurate description than this. It is the funeral that never ends.

I confess, I hate divorce. I hate what it does to people. I hate how it makes enemies of those who once declared undying love for one another. But I especially hate the damage it does to children.

Now don't misunderstand me. The majority of my readers here will most likely be those who are divorced or are divorcing. I would hate to think that the expression of such strong feelings is making you feel worse or that I am piling up fuel for your guilt by such strong remarks. But divorcing is not as benign a life event as some modern-day soothsayers would have us believe. I merely want to remind you that you need to pay particular attention to your children throughout. If you don't, they will be the ones to suffer

Furthermore, let me say that divorce is inevitable and unfortunately often unavoidable in a fallen and broken world. Everyone makes mistakes. People change and turn out not to be who you thought they were when you married them. While I believe that everything possible must be done to try and preserve marriage, divorces will happen. Many divorced parents are not the instigators of their divorces, nor did they choose this state. They are the innocent victims of someone else's sin and would have tried again to make their marriages work if they had been given the chance. Marital dissolution is a tragic, but sometimes unavoidable, consequence of our humanness and sin. So try to move beyond feeling unnecessary and prolonged guilt over your mistakes. Take God's forgiveness and move on. Try to focus on what you can do to bring healing to all the parties concerned, especially the children.

There is so much that divorcing parents can do to prevent damage to their children. To deny that divorce is damaging will probably do more harm than anything else because such denial excuses parents from try ing to help their children.

I am sorry to say that my profession has been as guilty of such divorce soothsaying as any. And since divorcing parents often, if not always, feel guilty about what they are doing, they eagerly accept the placating platitudes of those who say, "Don't worry about it. The kids will get over it quickly; it's amazing how resilient they are." Is this true? I don't think so, and my purpose here is to lay out in this chapter the data as clearly as possible.

While I do not want to create problems where none exists, I do believe it is time we evaluated the consequences of divorce on children more honestly. I think it is important for motivating parents to work at taking positive and constructive steps to reduce the damaging effects of divorce on children.

Some Children Are Resilient

First let me concede that one cliché often bandied about in divorce circles is that some children can go through divorce without a scratch. They are resilient and bounce back easily. As far as we can see, there is little noticeable effect on their later lives. They have strong, healthy egos, built from the early days of their lives by loving, though separated, parents. They have been taught the necessary controls and psychological safety valves that enable them to release built-up tensions without becoming overwhelmed or immobilized.

But it is a mistake to think that such resilience came about naturally, that the parents themselves did nothing to foster it. When left to themselves, children suffer the greatest damage.

It is also a mistake to assume that resilient children experience no pain whatsoever, or that they are strong and courageous all the time! Remember, a resilient child isn't necessarily the one who never cries or shows pain. The avoidance of pain is a sure sign of nonresilience. So it is not necessarily a bad sign for a child to cry a lot or to act weak and upset.

Also, the immediate reaction to the announcement of a divorce can be very misleading. The resilience I am talking about here is something that develops over a long time. It may not seem to be there at the time of the divorce.

It is safe to assume, therefore, that whether a child seems resilient or not, or appears emotionally healthy or not, that divorce will always have some damaging effects. The question is whether or not it will be short-lived or have long-term consequences. And here is the good news: It all depends on you, the parents. You can determine the outcome for good.

The assumption that there is always some damage can keep parents from neglecting the positive steps that can be taken to help the child. Don't play denial games with your children's pain.

The Evidence for Long-Term Damage

The evidence supporting the belief that divorce can damage children if not handled properly is overwhelming, and I need to pause here to draw attention to it if only to convince those parents who would still prefer to believe that divorce is harmless.

The evidence is so overwhelming that I hardly know where to begin. Since this is not the place to be highly technical, allow me to highlight the key findings. The reader who wants more can find it in the references I will give.

The classic study that raised our awareness of what divorce does to all parties is that of Judith Wallerstein and her colleagues at the California Children of Divorce Project. (See *Second Chances: Men, Women, and Children a Decade after Divorce*, by Judith Wallerstein and Sandra Blakeslee, published by Tickner and Fields, New York, 1989.) Wallerstein's longitudinal studies go back many years and give a long-term view of how divorce damages children. Despite those critics who have persisted in finding fault with her work, it has stood the test of time.

Over a period of fifteen years, she and her colleagues have followed divorced families closely, their hopes, frustrations, fears, and disappointments. Every intimate detail has been observed.

What Wallerstein found was that significant numbers of children suffer for years from psychological and social difficulties after the divorce of their parents. What is more, these difficulties continued well into the adult lives of these children. They suffered from heightened anxiety, depression, social difficulties, achieving success, and in forming enduring attachments.

Despite the criticism that she did not have an adequate control group of nondivorced children to compare with, her findings have been replicated all over the world. In Finland, for example, another longitudinal study showed that divorced children had lower school performance, less education, more risky behavior, and more abundant negative life experiences. (See "Parental Divorce, Adolescence, and Transition to Young Adulthood," by Hillevi Aro and Ulla Palosaari, *American Journal of Orthopsychiatry;* July 1992, vol. 62(3), pp. 421–29.)

But let me hasten to add one very important observation about this research. I don't believe it has to turn out this way. Most of the divorcing parents in these studies did not seek or get help; they were not instructed on what to do or not do and were victims of their own resentment and helplessness.

So, while there is a consensus that divorce has the potential for much damage, I also know that given the right support with parents who quickly bring their hostility under control, the children of divorce can be preserved for a rich and meaningful life. And even if parents do make a lot of blunders, all is not lost. I managed to pull my life together in a meaningful way. What better testimony can I give than that!

One very special research project that does support my optimistic outlook here is from Canada. Researchers at the Calgary Family Service Bureau found that five factors could help children survive divorce better. These five factors are:

1. The personality healthiness of both parents
2. The quality of bonding between parents and children
3. The quality of attachment in the family
4. Parenting styles
5. The resilience of the child (see "The Impact of Divorce on Children," by Irmgard Thiessen, *The Journal of Early Child Development and Care,*" Dec. 1993, vol. 96, pp. 19–26)

These significant findings ALL point to the fact that children of divorce can be helped to achieve a better life.

How and Why Divorce Hurts Children

It also helps if parents know how and why divorce hurts children. This knowledge can help a parent avoid the pitfalls that strew the path to recovery.

A famous child psychologist, Dr. Lee Salk, once said: "The trauma of divorce is second only to death. Children sense a deep loss and feel they are suddenly vulnerable to forces beyond their control." This statement agrees completely with my experience as a clinical psychologist. Never again will most of the children of divorce ever have to face as stressful a life event. The acute stress of the shock, the intense fears of the unknown, the feelings of uncertainty and insecurity, and the need to grieve over the loss of the traditional family structure are enough to bring the strongest of us to our knees.

Among the more important reasons why divorce is damaging to children are the following:

- It signals the collapse of the family structure—the child feels alone and very frightened. This loneliness can be acute and long remembered.
- Parents have a diminished capacity to parent. They are preoccupied with their own emotions and survival during the critical months (or years) of the divorce.
- The divorce creates conflicts of loyalty in the children. Whose side do they take? Often children feel pulled by love and loyalty in both directions.
- Uncertainty about the future causes deep-seated insecurity. Being dependent mainly on one parent creates a great deal of anxiety.
- The anger and resentment between the parents, which is so prevalent in most divorces, creates intense fear in the child. The younger the child, the more damage this climate of hostility can do.

- Children take on much anxiety over their parents. They worry intensely about their mother, in particular, with the departure of the father (or the father, if it is the wife who leaves).

- If the family moves, a child may lose an at-home parent, a home, a school, neighborhood, church, and friends. Divorce represents a loss of so many things that a deep depression is almost unavoidable in children. Most parents fail to recognize this depression.

- Most children of divorce suffer from economic descent after divorce. Divorce makes all the parties, but especially the wife, poorer. Divorced women are the new impoverished members of our society.

The Effect of Divorce on the Stages of Childhood

One of the clearest messages coming to us from the researchers is that the impact of divorce is selective. Both the timing of the divorce and the age of the children are important factors that determine the outcome.

This makes sense. Maturity is a function of age, so the more mature a child is, the better he will be able to deal with the changes that divorce demands. Timing and age are crucial to the outcome.

Common as divorce is in our society now, few children are really prepared for it when it happens. They expect it to happen to their friends, not to them. About 80 percent of children receive no warning that a divorce is about to take place. Even if the news is broken slowly and gently, the reaction is nearly always the same (and just as I personally experienced it when my parents divorced): shock, followed by denial, then anger, fear, lowered self-esteem, and depression. Many children also develop a haunting suspicion that they may have been responsible for their parents' problems. I know I did!

But how do children of different ages respond? Here is a summary:

- *Toddlers* (two to four years of age) often show signs of regression to an earlier stage of development. They become more dependent and passive, engaging in babyish behavior.

Rather than feeding themselves, they demand that you feed them, and they revert to a need for diapers even though they may already be potty-trained. Some psychologists feel that the absence of the parent of the opposite sex at this stage may be detrimental to a child's sexual development,.

* *Young children* (five to eight years of age) also regress. In addition, these children tend to take responsibility for the marriage breakup. They tend to have irrational fears of being abandoned and even of starving. These fears need to be confronted and appropriate assurances given. Loss of sleep, bedwetting, nail-biting, a deep sense of sadness (often a masked depression), and a retreat into fantasy as a way of solving the family crisis are all likely to occur at this age.

    Some authorities believe that this age—when the child is old enough to know what is going on but not old enough to have adequate skills for dealing with it—is the most critical age for children to experience divorce.

* *Older children* (nine to twelve years of age) experience anger as the dominant emotion. This anger is usually directed at the parent believed to be the initiator of the breakup, but it is easily scapegoated outside of the family and directed at peers just at a time when the support of loving friends is most needed. Children may alienate those close to them—including teachers and close relatives.

    The spiritual development of the child is most likely to be damaged at this age. Disappointment, disillusionment, and rejection of the parents' spiritual values could easily occur. "They are just hypocrites and I don't want to have anything to do with their religion," is a very common reaction.

* *Teenagers* (thirteen years of age and over) have a different set of problems to deal with. They tend not to assume blame for the divorce as readily as younger children do because they have a better understanding of the reasons for the divorce. Nevertheless, they can also be deeply hurt and resent their

parents for breaking up the home. They fear being separated from their friends, and as there is a natural tendency toward withdrawing and feeling depressed at this age, a divorce could accentuate these problems. It is common for them to isolate themselves and refuse to talk about what's bothering them.

Teenagers also feel the "loyalty dilemma" acutely. They know that mother doesn't want them to like their father (or vice versa). "How can you like someone who has done this terrible thing to me?" or "Don't you know what a terrible person he (or she) is?" is typical of parental attitudes that create conflicts for teenagers. Keeping the peace with both parents can be emotionally draining for them.

Which of the Sexes Suffers Most

There is no doubt in the minds of many psychologists that boys are harder hit by divorce than girls. The reasons are not hard to discern: Boys are taught in our culture not to show painful emotions. They are told "Boys don't cry; boys have got to be MEN." Boys, therefore, tend to deny their negative emotions more than do girls; this denial can be the source of the emotional constrictiveness many men exhibit later in life.

More is expected of boys in these circumstances, especially by fathers who feel guilty. They are expected to be stronger, more resilient, more capable of taking care of themselves, but this is not necessarily true. When their defenses break down, boys are often more devastated than girls are.

While boys are considered to be at greater risk, there is now a growing body of evidence that it is changing for girls. The disengagement of divorced fathers from their daughters is becoming a really serious concern. The daughters of divorce are now evidencing delayed effects, consequences that may only show up when they marry. In other words, they experience the onset of their problems much later than boys. The truth is, that girls need a father as much as a boy does. Never believe otherwise!

Remarriage and Stepfamilies

Much attention is being given to stepfamilies, often referred to as *reconstituted* or *blended* families. Incorporating a new husband or wife, or finding yourself with instant brothers and sisters through remarriage, superimposes a whole new set of challenges on the children. The second time around for them is not always a bed of roses.

Adjusting to life between two homes, often in reduced financial circumstances, is complicated and confusing enough for a child without the added intrusion of an unwanted stepparent. In retrospect, I think I was fortunate in having a stepfather (although he never called himself this) who had not been previously married and had no children of his own. I only had him to contend with, not a slew of forced siblings to boot!

To make matters worse, a divorced parent, especially the mother, may not be in the right state of mind to make a wise choice about a new mate. While it is a good idea to wait at least a year before remarrying, many don't. They move too quickly into a second marriage without having resolved the residual problems from the first. This can be disastrous for both the wife and the children.

And then there are the economic consequences of divorce. For instance, the costs of litigation and maintaining two households can reduce a family's income enormously. A Census Bureau report reveals that only 25 percent of divorced or separated mothers receive child support. This figure is now rising dramatically. So, many single mothers rush into a second marriage merely to escape financial insecurity or diminished status—hardly the right reason to get married! Under these conditions mistakes are easily made, and the risk of a second marriage ending in divorce is very high.

Some Divorces Are Worse than Others

No two divorces are identical. The nature, circumstances, and reasons for a divorce are varied.

Not all divorces are equally damaging to children. One critical issue is the hostility factor. The rule is simple to remember: The greater the hostility, the greater the damage.

Where a divorce is pursued impulsively or in anger, or where the divorce coincides with other unrelated family crises, a child's capacity to cope will be seriously impaired and more damage results.

The most damaged children are those involved in custody battles or where the war between the parents goes on forever. Easily duped into switching loyalties, these children are swayed by appeals for loyalty and are often seduced by ridiculous promises from either parent. "You can have your own telephone if you come and live with me," "I'll buy you a new bicycle," or "I'll give you a large allowance" are typical bribes often used by parents to win over the child's allegiance.

These battles are seldom carried out with the child's best interest in mind. They are nearly always selfish and an extension of the basic marital conflict that started it all. Frequently it is a way of taking revenge and punishing the other parent.

Caught in the crossfire of such vindictive competition and this tug-of-war, children can be scarred for life. And even the most skillful psychotherapist may not be able to put little Johnny or Mary together again!

Many custody cases, of course, are not that severe. But children are hurt by divorce even under the best of circumstances, and many do not bounce back nearly as quickly as they are expected. As a matter of fact, studies show that, among children whose parents divorce, 37 percent are still depressed five years later. Depression becomes a permanent part of life for many children of divorce.

Is the Dissolution of the Family Sometimes Good for Children?

This is a valid question and worthy of consideration. Many wives or husbands are sometimes confronted with the dilemma of seeing destruction at work in their children because of a hostile marriage or a destructive parent. What are they to do? It is common for them to ask, therefore, whether a family being dissolved isn't sometimes a relief for the children involved.

Yes, there are times when the damage being done to children is so bad that it is in the best interest of the children that a family no longer stay together. These instances are rare and I will mention them later. Notice, however, that I am careful to say that the family shouldn't stay together. *I am not saying that a divorce is the best solution.* Divorce is a separate issue, and this book is not about when and when not to divorce. However, parents may decide to live apart for the sake of their children when the destruction, such as that caused by incest or abuse, far outweighs the benefits of being together.

The majority of divorces do not fit this category. So when you ask the children of divorce whether the breakup was in their best interest or not, the majority say no. Less than 10 percent report being relieved by their parents' divorce, and those children who do feel relieved still seem to have difficulty adjusting to the consequences of the divorce.

Far from being happy about their parents' divorce, most children—even those from quite troubled homes—seem willing to put up with almost anything or go to any length to keep their parents together. In fact, across all ages and both sexes in the children of divorce is the common fantasy that somehow, somewhere, miraculously, the parents will reunite. There seems to be an instinctive urge to keep the family together. I know I felt it!

True, this fantasy sometimes develops as a way of alleviating the anxieties surrounding divorce, but the fantasy stays alive for many years, way beyond the anxiety phase. I can recall thinking, as late as ten years after my parents were divorced, "Wouldn't it be wonderful to have my children experience a united pair of grandparents as I did when I was a child!"

Sometimes fantasies of reuniting parents lead children to engage in bizarre behavior in order to bring about such reconciliation. One young child I dealt with would repeatedly take the hands of her parents when they were together and place them on top of each other. Another nine-year-old would deliberately expose herself to the bitterly cold winter's air with hardly any clothes on to try and get sick so her parents would have to take care of her together. One twelve-year-old boy told me that he often prayed that he would die so that his parents would each blame themselves, feel guilty, and reunite. Such is the power of this instinct!

But children eventually learn that such tactics don't work and move on to acceptance. But the strong desire to reunite the family helps to shed light on the question: Should an otherwise normal but unhappily married couple abide by the old-fashioned wisdom of "remaining married for the good of the children," or follow the modern wisdom of our so-called liberated thinking that an unhappy couple might well divorce, also "for the good of the children"?

I suppose that either rule, applied simplistically and without consideration of the complex nature of marriage, can lead to disaster. One is not universally superior to the other. And it is true that where there is continuous, severe conflict with physical abuse, the damaging effects on children may be so serious, they outweigh the damage that divorce itself brings.

On the whole, however, my experience as a psychotherapist and the available research leads me to believe that, when it is at all possible, trying to save the existing marriage by getting appropriate help is infinitely preferable to trying a second or third one. This course of action is far more likely to lead to a fulfilling and satisfying life for all the parties concerned. And I say this quite apart from the theological or moral implications of divorce that every Christian couple must face!

Does Divorce Solve Everything?

People opt for divorce for complex reasons, and some of these reasons have little or nothing to do with marriage compatibility. Boredom, falling in love with somebody else, poor communication habits, irrational ideas about what one or the other partner wants from life, middle-age crises, and personal neuroses are more frequently the real reasons why a marriage breaks up. The deep-seated, fundamental incompatibility reason is not the real reason. I say this because incompatibility is the given, not the exception. Ask my adorable wife!

For this reason I believe that most marriages can be saved and turned into satisfying relationships if both partners commit themselves to making the marriage work, and if both are willing to get help and do some changing. If I didn't believe this, I would quit what I do for a living.

Unfortunately, however, in our culture we have long been the victims of seductive, romanticized notions about marriage. We have been duped into looking at marriage only on the level of a relationship in which we believe certain needs (mostly neurotic and irrational) must be met. When they are not met, our culture tells us, we have a right to end the marriage.

Premier among these distorted and fantasized needs are, of course, our sexual needs. Unfortunately our culture (and this includes our Christian subculture) has created a neurotic monster in sexual disguise. Most married people are chasing a sexual satisfaction they mistakenly believe exists outside themselves. Disillusionment will be the result, because real satisfaction always lies within oneself. (See my book *The Sexual Man*, Word Publishing, 1994, for a more complete discussion.)

In the contemporary view of marriage, commitment and sacrifice are archaic words that no longer have meaning. In the process of losing our family values, we have also lost the ability to really love and achieve contentment and deep happiness.

Contrary to what our culture has led us to believe, however, divorce is not the only answer to an unhappy marriage. I am convinced that the solution to most miserable marriages is to be found in creative counseling, sound marriage guidance, and, if necessary, individual therapy for the marriage partners—as well as in a mutual turning to God in repentance and calling on him for help and healing.

I do not buy the simplistic notion that divorce will solve all our marital problems, because I have seen too many instances in which divorce has created more problems than it solved. Research backs me up on this point. Of adults who are surveyed five years after their divorces, only about a quarter are "resilient," that is, they are managing to cope adequately with their new lives. Half are muddling along, just barely coping. And the final quarter are either failing to recover or looking back with intense longing to the time before their breakups, wishing the divorce had never taken place. Far from taking care of all their problems, these divorces had just added a whole set of new ones.

Are You Sure You Must Get Divorced?

Much of what I have just written is designed to cause Christian parents to pause and reconsider their decision to divorce. I have deliberately avoided theological or moral arguments against divorcing, not because I don't believe there are scriptural reasons for staying married, but because I believe the damaging consequences of divorce and the rights of children to live a life free of conflict are so overwhelming as to reinforce scriptural injunctions against the easy divorce espoused in our culture today.

Nevertheless, divorce does happen and continues to split families at an alarming rate in Christian circles. The number of children involved in divorce has tripled in the last twenty years, and dealing with divorce is no less traumatic for children today than it was when I was a child.

If you are considering divorce, it is my hope and prayer that you will seriously consider the following suggestions before taking any further steps to end your marriage:

1. Examine again the following scriptural admonitions about divorce. Read Matthew 5:31–32, Matthew 19:3–9, Mark 10:2–12, Luke 16:18, Romans 7:1–3, and 1 Corinthians 7:10–17.

2. Seek another perspective on what is wrong with your marriage. Perhaps YOU are the problem, and another marriage will not change this. Talk to your pastor. He or she can refer you to a marriage counselor, psychologist, or family psychiatrist, depending on the nature of your problem.

3. Be honest and willing to confront your own contribution to the problems in your marriage. Seldom is a marriage problem caused by only one party.

4. Challenge the simplistic idea that getting divorced "will solve all my problems." Consider the consequences carefully and be skeptical of friends who push you to divorce, especially if they are also divorced. Often this is simply their way of getting you to join them and relieving their own guilt.

5. Accept the fact that all marriages have problems and that all relationships go through seasons. A "winter" now may mean a more glorious "spring" is just around the corner. You loved your spouse once; it can happen again. In particular, don't let unforgiveness get in the way. If your spouse has done

something really terrible, then remember that you are obligated to forgive him or her no matter how bad the deed.

6. Above all, pray for patience, determination, wisdom, and courage; God is waiting to give these to you. Claim what is yours by birthright!

7. Take the initiative to seek a solution to your marital problems. Go to a counselor by yourself, if necessary.

8. Remember that love and hate are not opposites. Love and hate are two sides of the same coin, they always intermingle. Whomever you love, you also have a great capacity to hate!

9. Remember: all that it really takes to make a marriage work is *commitment and a willingness to change!*

If your marriage can't be saved or if you are already divorced, then I trust the chapters that follow will be of help as you seek to turn your tragedy into an experience that promotes growth and maturity for you and your children. With just a little extra effort you can help your children to build a more solid, secure, and happy life for themselves.

CHAPTER 3

Healing Your Resentment

Approximately one-third of divorced parents, according to research, remain bitter and hostile several years after separation. This agrees with my own clinical experience. It is called "the parental alienation syndrome." It is the curse that dogs most divorces.

What's the problem with this syndrome? It is always the children who are at greatest risk for emotional damage. They get wounded by the crossfire of the war that never ends! If you really care about your children, you will make it your highest priority to heal the hostility and resentment created by your unhappy marriage and strife-riddled divorce.

Healing always begins with yourself. It doesn't matter how disturbed your ex-spouse is or who was to blame for the marriage breakup. YOU are the starting point for all healing. If you wait for your spouse to begin, you may just have a very long wait!

Before you, as a divorced parent, can begin to help your child build a stronger personality to withstand the onslaught of pain, you must begin to heal the resentment that you will unavoidably build up through your divorce.

This is not to say that healing is a once-only event. Healing is a process; it will take time to accomplish. Since it is a process, it must have a beginning and, thank God, an end. It can be accelerated, even if you cannot see that end now. All it takes is a little determination, some self-honesty, a measure of courage, and a strong conviction that it is imperative for you to resolve your hurt, hate, and need for revenge as soon as possible. It is like finding out you have a cancerous tumor. The sooner you act to remove it, the better the outcome will be.

Perhaps you don't think you have any hurt or resentment. Perhaps you have convinced yourself that there is nothing to feel resentment about. If this is true you are a very rare person, even quite extraordinary. I am not suggesting that you are not being completely honest with yourself, just that I have never met anyone like you! It is more likely that you are avoiding these feelings because you are afraid that they might get the better of you, or because you don't really know what to do with them. This chapter is designed to help you confront these feelings head on and overcome them.

Who Hurts the Most in a Divorce?

In every divorce there are two parties: the one who initiates the divorce and the one who gets divorced. Rarely, though it does happen, do couples get divorced by absolute, genuine, mutual feelings of relief, with no hurt to either party. Mostly, one hurts more than the other.

If there are children, of course, they are also hurt, often deeply. It is my purpose here to show parents how to minimize this hurt and how to heal whatever pain cannot be avoided.

There are others who also get hurt: parents, relatives, and friends. It is nearly impossible to contain the ripple effects of hurt in divorce. For our purposes here, however, I will focus on the two main parties involved— the partner who is rejected and the children. I would encourage the rejecting partner to read this chapter to understand how you can help in the healing of the children.

Seldom, if ever, is divorce a benign life-experience for both partners. One reads of strangers marrying for one party to gain immigration status or to capture an inheritance. These stories make wonderful movie plots. "Get married or you don't inherit," a will says. So Johnny-Who-Can't-Commit finds someone who goes along for the ride. The parties then get divorced as soon as the estate pays out or immigration status is assured, without ever getting to know each other. Also, I suppose, there is no residual resentment. But if this really does happen outside the movies, it is not a real marriage.

In real life both parties may appear on the outside to mutually agree on divorce, but seldom is it free of feelings. Usually, deep down, at least one party would prefer not to divorce. The one who initiates the divorce usually feels guilty; the one being divorced feels rejected. Both the feelings of guilt and rejection can lead to resentment, but for different reasons.

But what is resentment? It is a deep feeling of displeasure and indignation from a sense of being injured or offended. This useless emotion pretty well covers a multitude of sins!

It is my clinical experience that the person being rejected is usually the one who suffers the most emotional pain in divorce. The exception might be the partner who has been violated by infidelity and who then feels that he or she must depart the marriage. Here the one who is rejecting carries resentment over what caused the breakdown of trust, not so much over the divorce itself.

No one enjoys rejection. We are not built for it. Our souls crave acceptance. If there is to be a dissolution of a relationship, we prefer it if WE do the rejecting. There is less soul damage this way.

The bottom line is that the person who feels the most hurt will be the one to experience the most resentment. So, even if you don't deserve the hurt and are completely innocent, this chapter is for you. Healing must begin where the greatest damage has been experienced. So don't say things like "Well, if he will take the first step I will stop my resentment" or "If she will forgive me I will let go of my anger." For your own sake, start with yourself!

The point I am making is that resentment is present in almost every divorce and can be assumed to exist, to some degree, in all the parties involved. This resentment must be healed before any progress can be made in helping the children of divorce.

Why Must We Eradicate All Resentment?

I would have thought that the answer to this question was obvious, but so many of my patients resist the whole idea of getting rid of resentment that I need to address the issue here. Many struggle to come up with the motivation needed to get rid of their resentment.

For starters, let me point you to the apostle Paul, who, under the inspiration of the Holy Spirit, gave the following instruction: "Get rid of all bitterness, rage and anger, brawling and slander, along with every form of malice" (Ephesians 4:31 NIV). This sounds like a pretty clear message to me.

But we can go further. Getting rid of your resentment is crucial to the well-being of your children. All feelings of resentment must be resolved as soon as possible after a divorce if any good is to come of it. This is seldom accomplished before divorce proceedings begin, because the very process of divorce is in itself traumatic and resentment-producing. I have known many marriages where the partners appear to have it all together going into the preliminary proceedings and then fall apart when the divorce becomes a reality. And it isn't always lawyers who escalate the conflict.

There is a further reason why it is crucial to resolve resentment as soon as possible. Almost certainly, an endless round of quarrels, disagreements, and skirmishes will occur over money, visiting rights, and in-laws. The postdivorce period demands as much adjustment as marriage does itself. A strong urge to hurt each other nearly always sets in after the divorce is finalized.

Now, I don't really care how much adults hammer away at each other. I've seen too much of it, and by and large the parents survive their private war. They are grownups and can fend for themselves! But when this ongoing conflict puts a damaging strain on children who are caught in the crossfire, my blood starts to boil! And, I am sorry to say, Christian parents are often guilty of this form of child abuse.

One so-called Christian mother who was in therapy with me felt so violated by her ex-husband that she became obsessed with thoughts about how to turn her children against him. She took every opportunity to tell them exaggerated stories about his extramarital exploits and about how he would withhold much-needed money for their personal needs. Every dirty detail of their past marriage was recounted again and again to her young children with damaging consequences. When I confronted her with how abusive this was to her children she exploded, "I *will* use my children against him! They must know what he's like. I want them to hate him as much as I do!"

I asked her, "What reason can you give to God for such vitriolic misuse of your parental privilege?" Her answer?

"I thought I would punish my husband through my children because I'm not sure God will do such a good job of it!"

Actually, she's right. It is very possible God won't punish him at all if he repents. God is like that, and it infuriates people who know nothing of his grace.

Divorced Christian parents are most open to sin when they are driven by the destructive power of resentment. This is why healing from resentment should be the first priority for the Christian parent who is divorced. There is no excuse for anyone here.

Resentment: The Cancer of the Emotions

Resentment is not an emotion psychologists like to talk about much. I recently scanned through the indexes of a dozen fairly new introductory psychology textbooks on my bookshelf. In none of these was I able to find any reference to the emotion of resentment. In fact, I believe that outside the Christian gospel there is no real solution to the problem of resentment! Psychology by itself certainly does not have a solution. The reason I say this will become obvious as I proceed. Only the gospel of Christ is capable of healing the deepest human hurt at its very root.

Many believe that resentment is the most destructive of all human emotions. Its damage is felt not only in the psyche but also in the depth of our souls. It is as much a spiritual problem as it is a psychological one, and its solution lies in both the spiritual and the psychological realms.

Its destructive power comes from several sources:

- Resentment has a perfect memory—it never forgets.
- Resentment exaggerates all subsequent hurts.
- Resentment destroys happiness and prevents contentment.
- Resentment has only one human cure—revenge.

I will explore each of these destructive sources in the remainder of this chapter.

Why We Cling to Resentment

One of the brain's most fascinating mechanisms, and the one that keeps us sane, is our ability to forget. I believe that God deliberately created us with a memory that fades.

I know we complain about this when we can't recall a name or an address, but believe me, forgetfulness is a great blessing as well as a great healer. It protects the mind from becoming overcrowded with unnecessary details.

If we never forgot (and think of how much happens to a person in just one day), we would go crazy. Our conscious storage capacity would very soon be all taken up, and the brain, large enough as it is, would run out of space.

The unfortunate thing about resentment is that it refuses to let the healing power of forgetting do its work. It keeps the memory of our hurts alive for a long time. These memories, in turn, recreate for us, day by day, the pain we experienced and a need to get even—a strong desire for revenge.

I marvel at the ability of the human mind to carry resentment almost indefinitely. I don't see this in my cat; he seems to forget injustices almost right away. If I forget to feed him, it is all forgotten the moment I do feed him. Amazing! Animals are incapable of bearing grudges. Perhaps this is why so many people love their pets more than they do other people!

But when we humans are violated or hurt we don't forget so easily. This is why, in Old Testament times, God set aside forty-eight cities in Israel to be used as "cities of refuge." It was to these cities, scattered throughout Israel, that those who had committed involuntary manslaughter could flee to escape the wrath of the dead person's relatives and friends. The "eye for an eye and tooth for a tooth" principle prevailed in Old Testament law, so even a person who unintentionally took another's life could be punished with death. Those who escaped to one of the cities of refuge could remain there and be safe, but they could never leave again without fear of being punished.

Through the ages people have always retained the eye-for-an-eye tendency. It seems as if resentment burns itself indelibly into brain tissue because it best fits our "lower" natures. Do you know how hard it is to persuade someone to give up resentment? As a psychotherapist I have tried many times and failed. People cling to resentment as if their very lives depended on it!

The Way We Justify Resentment

Most of us hold on to resentment by convincing ourselves that our resentment is justified. We say to ourselves: "I have a right to feel this way. See how much I have been hurt?"

If you are like most people, no doubt you can point to many instances in your life where you have been traumatized, either physically or emotionally, and can recount many times when you were criticized or your love was rejected. You could prepare a display of your hurt that would convince the most skeptical jury that you have been unjustly treated. And you would be right! We are all wronged at some time in our lives. But does justifying yourself help you get rid of your resentment? Does it heal your wounds? I have yet to encounter any evidence that harboring resentment makes a person happier or healthier. On the contrary, resentment tends to destroy the one who holds on to it, not the one who committed the original injustice!

If resentment is so self-destructive, then why do we cling so tenaciously to it? I believe that when we hurt very deeply we actually, in some strange way, enjoy our resentment. It feeds self-pity; it makes us feel self-righteous. The nursing of resentment and planning for revenge resonates with very primitive survival needs; they are natural things for us to do. Alternatively, taking steps toward healing resentment feels uncomfortable, almost as if we are betraying our deepest existential needs. It takes courage, determination, and a dependence on God's help.

The Way We Accumulate Resentments

Resentment has a way of perpetuating itself; resentment breeds resentment just like weeds breed weeds.

One wife I was seeing in therapy found out that her husband was having an extramarital affair. When she confronted him with her discovery, he confessed the sordid business to her and asked for forgiveness.

She forgave him and for the first few months after the reconciliation the wife seemed to be handling her feelings well. But gradually, and without even realizing it, she began to find little things wrong with him. Slowly she accumulated memories of the petty hurts her husband caused her. Every time he did something that upset her, she added it to the memory of his unfaithfulness. After a few months she became super sensitive, even paranoid. She couldn't trust her husband. She spied on him whenever she could and even became suspicious about the way he dressed. "Why are you wearing that suit?" she would ask. "Why are you ten minutes late?" Resentment was breeding resentment, and very soon she was unable to control her feelings. Eventually her resentment led to the breakup of her marriage.

Another man felt he had been deeply harmed by his mother. When he was a little boy she would spy on him by barging into the bathroom when he wasn't expecting it.

When I met this man he was in his late forties and had become totally obsessed with his resentment about his mother who was now very old. He would bring letters she had written years before to prove what a horrible person she was. He even made tape recordings of telephone conversations with her to prove what a terrible person she was. Nothing I read or heard convinced me she was an ogre. His mother appeared to be a kind and gentle soul who was desperately trying to win her son's love. He twisted everything to justify and feed his resentment. The result? He became an obsessed and unhappy person. Resentment can poison our lives—as well as the lives of those around us.

How Should We Deal with Resentment

God did not intend that we become predisposed to self-destruction. As free-willed, fallen beings we choose our own destiny, and if left to our devices we would certainly self-destruct.

But God has not left us alone! He has provided a wonderful solution to our predicament—in the gospel. As a psychologist I continually marvel at how perfectly the gospel fits our needs and provides answers to our profoundest problems, even though we don't always avail ourselves of it.

As I reflect on God's healing provisions, especially for the healing of resentment, I see four important steps that must be taken to defuse the destructive power of resentment:

1. Develop a holy perspective on your hurts,

2. Dispose of your need for revenge,

3. Declare your forgiving spirit to those who have hurt you, and

4. Deliberately turn your resentment into kindness.

These steps are all consistent with a biblical perspective on how we should deal with hurt. Careful attention to each will bring healing to your resentment, and this in turn will make you more capable of helping your children overcome their own hurts. You, as a divorced parent, owe it to your children to provide the healthiest possible environment for them to adjust to their new condition. As we examine each of these steps in turn, rely on God to help you implement them in your life!

Develop a holy perspective on your hurts.

If we could effectively and rapidly forget our hurts, resentment would not be a problem. But we can't forget that easily. I sometimes joke about wanting our pharmaceutical companies to invent a "forgetting pill." I could sure use it in my clinical work!

Resentment, rather than helping us to forget, actually helps us remember. Hurt memories are kept alive, not helped to fade. So we must find another way to heal them.

There are no shortcuts here, even with God. He does not take our memories of hurt away but calls us to face them courageously.

Perhaps the most important thing to remember about hurt feelings is that we always feel the hurt in the here and now. If we are hurting now over something that happened last week, it is because our memories can still vividly recall the facts of the hurt. So make a note of the following rule: *The healing of our resentment begins when our memories lose their ability to recreate the feeling of hurt in the present.* Believe me, this is a powerful rule!

How do we take away from our memories their ability to hurt us? One way is to learn to look at our hurts in the context of the hurt we cause God by our waywardness. Jesus told a very important parable, often referred to as the "parable of the unforgiving servant," in Matthew 18:21–35. As with all Jesus' parables, it contains a powerful message from God.

The parable starts with Peter asking Jesus how often he is to forgive his "brother" who sins against him. Is seven times enough?

Jesus replies that it has to be more than this, in fact even seven times seven isn't enough. He then tells the story of a king who wanted to balance out his servants' accounts. One servant brought to him owed him a thousand talents (almost a million dollars in our money). When told to pay up, he pleads on his knees with the king not to sell his wife, children, and all he had. "I promise, I will pay all my debt. Just give me a little more time."

How does the king respond? He is moved with compassion and forgives him all his debt.

As this servant leaves the king's chambers he encounters a second servant who owes him a hundred pence (about ten dollars). Taking him by the throat he demands, "Pay me now or else!" The second servant falls on his knees pleading, "I promise, I will pay all my debt. Just give me a little more time." The unforgiving servant refuses and has him imprisoned until he can pay the debt.

When the king hears of this he calls the first servant back and says: "O thou wicked servant, I forgave thee all that debt, because thou desiredst me: Shouldest not thou also have had compassion on thy fellowservant, even as I had pity on thee? And his lord was wroth, and delivered him to the tormentors, till he should pay all that was due unto him."

Then Jesus says these very important words: "So likewise shall my heavenly Father do also unto you, if ye from your hearts forgive not every one his brother their trespasses."

I don't know about you, but these words of Jesus send shivers down my spine.

Now let's get the meaning of this parable clear. This is not a parable about money, but about hurts and resentments. Scripture refers to it as "being sinned against." And the characters? The king is God. The first servant is YOU. The second servant is the one who has hurt you. In our context here, your ex-spouse.

The key lesson is this: No matter how much others have hurt you (equivalent to ten dollars), your hurt is insignificant when compared to the hurt you have caused God (equivalent to one million dollars).

Now the punch line: Unless you forgive the hurt others have done to you, God cannot forgive your debt to him. It is as simple as that. I refer to it as the "fine print" of Scripture, because we tend to overlook it in our eagerness to be forgiven by God. But this formula is there in this parable. We pray it every time we pray the Lord's Prayer; "Forgive us our debts, as we forgive others . . ." You can't escape it!

Realizing this truth helps us to put our hurts in proper perspective. When we understand that the greatest hurt someone can cause us is nothing when placed alongside the hurt we cause God because of our waywardness and sinfulness, the question of how often we must forgive those who hurt us becomes irrelevant. There is no end to how often we must forgive, because our debt to God always remains greater than anyone else's debt to us, including an ex-spouse's. When we get this perspective clear in our minds, it is easier to let go of resentment.

Dispose of your need for revenge.

It is natural that when we are injured, we want to strike back. This tendency originates in our primitive need for self-preservation: "If you hurt me, I'll hurt you back."

In some situations this may be a healthy law, as for example when we are physically attacked. But when it comes to psychological hurts the need to retaliate is not helpful. It becomes self-destructive, not self-protecting. Revenge begets revenge, and there is no end to the cycle.

Susan, an intelligent and attractive woman in her midthirties, the mother of three children, discovered one day that her husband, Bob, was having an affair with her younger sister. She was outraged. Normally a rational and calm person, she suddenly discovered that she was capable of the most intense hatred. "I think I could even commit murder at this point," she told me when, after realizing how much her emotions could control her, she sought professional help.

Susan's situation was of the worst kind. "If only Bob had had his affair with someone I didn't know, it would be easier to forgive him. But my own sister! I have to face her almost every day. I can never forgive either of them."

For a while Susan carried her hurt and resentment deep within, concealed from everyone. Outwardly she gave the impression she had forgiven Bob and her sister, but at night, while trying to go to sleep, she would ruminate about the affair. She fantasized about coming in on her husband and sister and praying that God would destroy them both. She became irritable and angry at everyone. Slowly she became withdrawn and bitter. Her need for revenge now controlled her. "I think the only way I can rid myself of these feelings is to do something terrible to Bob and my sister," was her final, desperate conclusion.

To help Susan deal with her feelings of resentment, I reminded her of the parable of the unforgiving servant and asked her to put her hurt in perspective by placing it alongside the hurt she had caused God. My task for her was simply this: With God's help she was to come to the place where she could clearly see and understand that her hurt, terrible though it was, was insignificant compared to the hurt God could rightly feel about her.

This task took a little while. Susan prayed hard about it, and we prayed about it together. But slowly the full meaning of this truth dawned on her. She was able to get a larger vista on our fallenness. She was now ready for the next step—dealing with her strong desire for revenge.

I reminded her of the closing words of the parable as given in Matthew: "And so angry was the master that he condemned the man to torture until he should pay the debt in full. And that is how my heavenly father will deal with you, unless you each forgive your brother from your hearts" (Matthew 18:34–35, NEB).

How do we dispose of our need for revenge? By forgiving those who hurt us. THERE IS NO OTHER WAY! That is why non-Christians have no escape.

And what does it mean to forgive? Simply this: You surrender your right to retaliate. Humanly speaking, you have a right to hurt those who hurt you; revenge is an age-old principle! But when you forgive, according to God's way, you give up this right. Why? Because you need to be protected from the hurt. Giving up your right to revenge *is for your benefit*, because if you give in to your urge for revenge, there will be no end to the escalation of the conflict. God knows us all better than we know ourselves; that is why we are required to forgive.

After many years of dealing with the problems of people in the area of anger and resentment, I am more convinced than ever before that the healing of our "hurt memories" lies in forgiveness. As we willingly give up our need to hurt back, we take from the memory its power to hurt us.

In Susan's case, giving up her right to revenge was easy, though it is not always so for everyone. She just opened herself up to experience a fresh encounter with God's love and his grace. The next thing she realized was that she had found a new freedom from her resentment. Susan was a soul forgiven and set free again.

Declare your forgiving spirit to those who have hurt you.

While forgiveness is always necessary when dealing with resentment, it may not be sufficient. Not everybody hurts you just once, apologizes and asks for your forgiveness, and then never ever does it again. Sometimes people go on hurting you and hurting you! They may do it openly and maliciously, or they may do it unconsciously or inconspicuously. In either case the pain it causes can be excruciating.

What do you do in such a situation? Tell them clearly so that they know where you are coming from, that you will not allow their actions to make you bitter. You will not retaliate or take revenge. Rather than this giving them license to hurt you more, the reaction is usually to leave you alone.

Allow me to emphasize a point about forgiveness that is essential to the healing of resentment: Since forgiveness is designed to protect us from our own anger, it is not necessary for our enemies to admit their guilt or ask for our forgiveness. We give forgiveness, therefore, without regard to the attitude of the one who has hurt us.

Declaring your forgiving spirit doesn't mean you allow someone to go on hurting you. Having given forgiveness and declared it, you are then free to take the next step, which is to courageously ask whoever is hurting you to stop doing it. To do this you will need to be lovingly assertive and honestly confrontive.

You will need to risk revealing yourself here if you are going to succeed, and this may even increase your immediate risk of further hurt. In the long run, however, you are always the better for taking this risk.

Let us suppose that your spouse has divorced you. He declared he no longer loves you and wants to start life over with someone else. But it is now a year later, and to justify his actions he continues to drag up all your mistakes from the past or lists your many weaknesses. He takes every opportunity to brainwash your children into believing that he is good and you are bad and that he is doing the right thing. This behavior is driving you up the wall, and your resentment is escalating. What do you do?

Of course, your first step is to move yourself to a place of forgiveness. Don't retaliate. Surrender your right to get even. Then you are free to declare your rights and insist that the hurting stop.

But first a caution! The reason confrontation seldom works is that it usually becomes a vehicle for punishment. It is used to attack or humiliate the other person, and this never accomplishes its intended purpose. Remember, forgiveness comes first! Then calmly, courageously, and assertively—without hostility or rancor—stand up for your right not to be hurt any more.

Deliberately turn your resentment into kindness.

The healing of your resentment is not complete without this final step. Psychologists strongly emphasize the importance of "acting out" your beliefs as a way of strengthening them. In other words, if you behave as you would like to be, you can ultimately become what you want to be.

For instance, do you want to be a kinder person? Then start behaving more kindly toward others. You will find that the kindness eventually becomes a part of your whole being.

The apostle Paul gives us this same prescription for entrenching our healing from resentment. In Romans 12:17–21 he tells us never to yield to revenge because in so doing we will be overcome by evil. As an alternative he advises us to do the following: "Therefore if thine enemy hunger, feed him; if he thirst, give him drink: for in so doing thou shalt heap coals of fire on his head" (v. 20). Note that a divorced husband or wife clearly qualifies as an "enemy" here!

Paul's words merely echo what Jesus tells us in Matthew 5:44: "But I say unto you, love your enemies, bless them that curse you, do good to them that hate you ..."

Now, most people's reaction to these words would be "No way!" We have difficulty with these words because we are so preoccupied with the idea that those who hurt us are going to get away without being punished that we panic. We want revenge. We want to see our enemy punished. But the gospel has taken away our right to punish or see punishment done. God says, in effect, "I do the punishing around here; all I want you to do is to forgive. If you get that straight you can all live in peace."

Do you want to know how to free yourself from anger and resentment and obtain full advantage from forgiveness? Turn your resentment into kindness. React to an act of unkindness with a kindness. When you do this, what does it do for you?

- It helps you put your money where your mouth is! If you say you forgive, you had better behave as if you have forgiven.
- It reinforces your belief system by giving you the feeling that you are in control.
- It protects you from further anger and hostility.
- It maximizes the chance that the one who has hurt you will not continue to do so.
- It keeps you from further sin, because your behavior is in harmony with your attitudes.
- It places the blame for the conflict back where it belongs.

When we turn our resentment into kindness, we make sure that the coals of guilt and punishment are heaped over the head of the original guilty party. We keep our reaction from becoming a greater sin than the original action.

Human beings are complex creatures. This is what makes us so re-markable and beautiful. But we can only become beautiful within and fully functional when we obey the laws God has created and communi-cated to us. The rest of this book will only be helpful if you, as a divorced parent, start now to work at resolving your hurts and giving up your resentment. With God's help you can do it. Believe this with all your heart and mind. I've seen it happen in my life. It can happen in yours!

CHAPTER 4

Common Mistakes Made
by Divorced Parents

No two divorces are exactly alike. Often what works to alleviate destructiveness in one doesn't work in another. But the destructive divorces I have seen have had certain features in common, and it is these commonplace characteristics that I want to address here.

Parents who are divorcing or who are in the process of seeking a divorce tend to universally make the same mistakes. It is these mistakes that have the potential for causing great pain, and it helps to avoid them.

While no one is immune to bungling a matter as delicate as dissolving a marriage, the risk of making mistakes goes up under these circumstances. The painful emotions of divorce make everyone vulnerable to certain pitfalls.

Divorce is a highly charged emotional event that will test the character and best defenses of the strongest among us. You may be the most competent mother or artisan, the most skilled preacher or surgeon, and have every aspect of your life outside your marriage under perfect control. But the moment divorce takes over, the chances are high that it will bring out the worst in you and dredge up your weakest features. You easily become a bungling, clumsy idiot prone to all sorts of mistakes.

Because divorce brings out the worst in you, I would urge you to be totally honest with yourself and alert to the early signs of being out of control. So as I discuss the common mistakes that divorcing parents make, trust God to give you the wisdom to understand yourself. Don't be lulled into believing that you are doing the right thing, when in fact you are victimizing your children or destroying yourself.

Don't Condemn Yourself

Most normal parents earnestly try to do the best they can for their children. As a result we often feel that we have failed them. I know I do. Did I give them what they really needed growing up? Have I blown my parenting in some way? It is very natural for parents to feel that they have failed even when their children turn out to be wonderful.

Since this chapter is designed to point out the common pitfalls of divorce, it is bound to leave many readers feeling guilty in some respects. So at the outset let me appeal to you to use the discovery of your weak points as an impetus to growth, not as an occasion for self-condemnation. Failures are meant to help us grow—not push us into defeat. They are the feedback we need to show us where we have gone wrong and to point out the corrective steps we must take. When you fail, claim the forgiveness that God offers you for your human frailty, then rise up and change what you need to change. Make it your determination that you will learn from your mistakes, so that you can avoid making them the next time.

Since no two people will face the identical set of circumstances, and even if they do will not react the same way, there is some risk in my trying to tease out a common set of principles here So I am asking my reader to evaluate carefully whether my advice fits your situation or personality style and adapt it, if necessary, to your unique problems. Seek help from a professional if you cannot make any strategy work.

Don't Let Your Guilt Feelings Control You

It is the unusual parent who does not feel guilty over a divorce, whether you are the instigator or not. Sometimes you can feel guilty for what someone else is doing! When either or both of the parents are Christians, this feeling of guilt may even be greater. Why? There is a deep sense of not only having failed one's children but God as well.

It is important to point out here that there is a difference between feeling guilty and being guilty. You can both *feel* guilty and *be* guilty, but the two don't always go together. You can be guilty of a terrible outrage and yet not feel guilty at all. On the other hand, you can feel horribly guilty about something without actually being guilty of doing anything bad. For most people in our culture, our guilty feelings are always out of step with our actual guilt. The reason for this lies in the way our culture is always looking for someone to blame and in our own personality makeup.

Sometimes it is easy to recognize guilt feelings, but not always. Often one is totally unaware of how underlying guilt feelings can control one's behavior.

It is remarkable to me that despite our general psychological sophistication, simple but subtle feelings of guilt are not easily recognized. This would not be a problem if it didn't cause the damage it does.

Controlled as we are by guilt in our culture, divorced parents make the mistake of trying to alleviate the guilt they feel toward their children in a variety of ways. Parents try to appease their children with gifts or try to win them with outrageous promises. Discipline becomes a problem under these conditions, because parents are afraid to assert their authority for fear of hurting their children's feelings further. As a consequence, many parents become depressed. They feel helpless and unable to deal with the problems confronting them.

One young mother I knew had left her husband and two small children because she felt she was being trapped by the cultural stereotype of being a mother and housewife. She hated these roles and wanted to be free "to be her own person." For months afterward (it finally stretched to years) she would regularly send her children expensive gifts just to "show them I love them." She wouldn't visit them, claiming that such a visit would upset them. The truth is that she couldn't handle her guilt when with them. So she avoided seeing them altogether.

Despite the fact that she was a very intelligent person, this woman was unable to see how her guilt was controlling her. The gifts were not for her children's benefit, but for her own. She felt better when she sent them. Not visiting her children was to protect herself from guilt feelings, not to protect them from the pain of seeing her.

The ways we try to reduce our guilt feelings are legion, and any of them may crop up in a divorce situation. One parent may become over-generous and give in to a child's every request. Another may avoid responsibility or contact with his or her child, even moving to another part of the country to get away as far as possible to ease his or her feelings of guilt. Of course, all of these guilt-reducing tactics are both unfair and unfortunate for the child. They create confusion, distrust, and more pain in the child than they prevent in the parent.

What to Do with Your Guilt

Here are some suggestions for alleviating your guilt in a healthy way. I assume here that you are feeling guilty over something you are not actually guilty for. If you are doing something bad to your children, then it is appropriate that you feel guilty. Own it, correct your behavior, and the feeling of guilt will go away.

1. Try to find out why you are susceptible to guilt feelings. Did your parents cause you to feel a lot of guilt? A hangover from a very strict childhood can easily make you prone to extreme guilt feelings.

2. Be more open in acknowledging to someone else, someone close to you, your feelings of guilt. This helps you to get it out in the open where you can see how it is controlling you. Often we are reluctant to own such feelings for fear that we will have to change what we are doing. If we are doing something bad, then this is a legitimate fear. Guilt helps us correct faulty behavior. But since it is possible to feel guilty over many minor and irrelevant matters, we can best deal with these feelings by owning up to them to someone else.

3. Avoid playing games with yourself or others to relieve your guilt feelings. Guilt needs to be dealt with directly and

forthrightly. You need either to put right what is wrong or to accept God's forgiveness for it—or both.

4. Make a clear distinction in your mind between God's conviction and psychological feelings of guilt. It is easy to turn neurotic guilt into a god and thereby miss God's true prompting voice. Our consciences can't always be trusted. They are often controlled by forces that go back to our early childhood. It can be like some strict, overbearing, rigid parent.

One way you can tell the difference between false guilt feelings and God's conviction is how you respond to forgiveness. People who are controlled by inappropriate guilt feelings find it hard to accept forgiveness. They want to punish themselves by making themselves miserable. Those who are truly convicted by God respond readily to the forgiveness he provides.

The Absent Parent's Role Is Crucial

Often the absent parent, the parent who has left and does not live with his or her children, is not fully aware of how crucial his or her role is in the postdivorce period. Fathers, who most frequently are the absent parent, are the biggest culprits.

Research on the significance of the noncustodial parent shows clearly that contact reduces behavior problems, interparental conflict is low, and children do better at school. Who wouldn't want these benefits for their children?

One recent study interviewed children two years after their parents' divorce regarding their experiences and their feelings about it. At the same time they interviewed the divorced parents. The results are quite illuminating. They found that the parents were totally unaware of how intensely hurt the children still felt two years after the divorce. Additionally, about 30 percent of the children wished that they could have more contact with their absent parent.

Both these findings are relevant here. Because parents are out of touch with their children's feelings, they don't pay attention to what they need emotionally. This is especially true for the absent parent who isn't in touch anyway. It is easy for them to make the mistake of thinking it is better if they keep out of the way, but there is no evidence to support this. Children want and need ongoing contact with the absent parent.

Now let me hasten to add that while it cannot be categorically stated that a child who has contact with only one parent will inevitably be handicapped in his or her development, it is clear that those children who have a lot of contact with *both parents* are the least likely to be damaged by the divorce. This double contact keeps development on track. Where there is contact with only one parent, the custodial parent has to take extra steps to ensure the well-being of the child. This is where grandparents and other relatives play a crucial role.

It is imperative, therefore, that divorced parents make every effort to raise their children equally. Too often fathers abandon the parenting task to the mother, even in intact families. This has tragic consequences and should be avoided. But it is even more important that both divorced parents participate fully in the lives of their children. Living apart from the children does not excuse any parent.

Of course, if the absent parent is to be equally involved in raising the children, the parent with whom the children live must also make a special effort to make this possible. Here is the rub! Many custodial parents deliberately try to cut off the absent parent. Why? Mostly as punishment. But since the children are the losers, such behavior must be forestalled. Both parents must resolve their feelings of hostility and alienation so that adequate contact between the absent parent and the children can be ensured. If there is severe conflict between the spouses, it is probably good to arrange things so that contact between the absent spouse and the children does not take place in the presence of the custodial parent. *But there must be contact!*

Sometimes a well-meaning mother or father makes the excuse that the former spouse is totally unsuitable as a model for the children. While there may be rare instances, and I mean rare, in which this is true, I have generally found that this is just a rationalization to keep the hostile fires burning. Let me repeat: Children need to know that both their parents, even if one of those parents is not a perfect role model, are there for them. Amazingly, children are well able to decide for themselves whether a parent is a good role model. They reject parental role models as unsuitable when they have to, with one exception: If they are forced to avoid the other parent, they may be attracted to his or her lifestyle. Humans have this propensity for doing the opposite of what they are told. So don't be surprised if your enforced avoidance of the other parent backfires!

How an absent parent relates to his or her children is as important as the relationship itself. Just taking them for hamburgers and remaining emotionally distant is as bad as not seeing your children at all. The most effective way is to share common experiences. For instance, absent parents can go to church with their children on alternate Sundays, establish common interests such as hobbies or sporting activities, build models together, go to plays together (the movies just don't cut it), or take vacations together.

One absent father who hardly ever did anything during his marriage with his two boys, determined that he would be a better father now that he was out of the house. While he was married the conflict at home was so great that he preferred to keep away on weekends or holidays. After his divorce, however, he found a new freedom to be with his sons. But he soon realized that taking them to restaurants for meals, which was what visiting day had degenerated to, did not satisfy him or his boys. So he decided to purchase a small sailboat and learn to sail. He taught his boys how to sail and this shared recreational activity revolutionized their relationships. It provided a common point of contact and interest, and over the years firmly bonded father and sons like nothing else could.

Another father, after his divorce, saw an opportunity to share an interest in stamp and coin collecting with his ten-year-old daughter. The young girl had started collecting stamps and coins a year before the divorce, and the father, with the intention of building a better relationship, decided that he would also take up the hobby. The hobby eventually became as much of a passion for him as it was for his daughter. More importantly, it gave them a shared interest.

Finding common points of interest is not difficult and doesn't have to cost money. All it takes is a commitment and a little ingenuity. The local library is full of ideas about hobbies and other fun activities parents and children can do together. Attending your child's soccer or other games, picking up your children from school, walks, picnics . . . The list is endless.

Visitation Rights—The Nightmare

More conflict arises over visitation rights than over any other aspect of a divorce, barring money. The conflict usually stems from inflexibility on the part of one of the parents. Usually visitation rights are used to manipulate, to gain some advantage, or to punish the ex-spouse.

Whatever the reason, *it is always the child who suffers from these conflicts.* It is unfair to a child for either or both parents to allow this to happen. Conflicts over visitation rights create tension and always mar the quality of the visit—which is probably what one of the parents intends to happen.

Depriving a child of a visit to the other parent is sometimes used to punish the child, often as an unconscious way of punishing the other parent. "Just for being sassy, you're not going to see your father tomorrow." Who really suffers here? Does the custodial parent really think that this form of punishment really changes behavior? It is more likely to build up resentment that will reap its dues later.

Obviously, this is a poor choice of punishment. While it may be very effective in the short run, it strikes at the root of the child's need for security and is destructive to his or her emotional health. Using such a punishment is, in the long run, self-defeating for the parent.

The visits of a child to his or her other parent should be treated with great respect, no matter what your feelings are. Your child's respect for you will grow by leaps and bounds. One of the reasons I have such great respect for my stepfather, more than for my own father, is that he always respected and encouraged my visits to my father. I can never recall otherwise!

A host parent who has difficulty with this should seek professional help as soon as possible. These visits are so crucial to a child's well-being that nothing must interfere with them.

A very common mistake parents make regarding visitation rights is to interrogate their children after a visit about the ex-spouse's affairs. Children despise being used as spies. This is as bad as it gets in a divorce. One teenager, named Tom, expressed it to me this way: "I hate it when my mother asks me questions about my father. I scream at her and tell her to stop it. It's the same with my father; it gets to the point where my father will tell me things and say, 'Don't tell your mother,' and I don't like to lie. But when my mother asks me a straight-out question, I have to lie. I'm not going to tell her because I know it will hurt her. And if I did tell her, my father would find out and get mad at me. It all drives me crazy!"

I know how you feel, Tom. It's a living hell!

Another pair of teenagers (they are, in fact, twins, brother and sister) told me of a game they would play with their mother. Their story goes like this: "Sometimes she'll get on our nerves and ask questions like, 'Is your stepmother pregnant?' So I would say no while my sister said yes, then we'd switch and I'd say yes and my sister no. We'd keep this up till Mom got mad and stopped asking us questions. She realized she wasn't going to get anything out of us."

Children also resent being asked to carry messages. The most common message is, "Ask your father to give you the check" or "Ask your father why I haven't gotten the check." This forces the child to be the carrier of guilt-inducing messages to the other parent and sets up conflict between the child and the other parent. You always get clobbered for bringing bad news!

This may, of course, be the home parent's unconscious intention, or the home parent may be totally unaware of the damaging effects such a practice has on the child's relationship. Either way, don't send messages through your children; these are issues parents should work out between themselves.

Change Things Slowly

If I were to single out the most serious mistake that divorcing parents make, it would be this: You change things too quickly.

The longer I practice as a psychotherapist the more convinced I become that people can tolerate slow change better than fast or sudden change. When change takes place slowly we learn to adapt to it more easily and make the necessary adjustments more effectively.

This means that right from the moment when divorce is being contemplated, both parents need to give a lot of thought to the speed with which changes are made. For example, it is quite common for the rejected spouse to want to run away. It is the panic mode of survival. "I'm going to sell everything and move to Alaska (or Timbuktu or wherever)!" Or "I'll move back to my hometown!" And many do just that. They pack up and move just to be able to avoid the pain of staying where they are. The mistake is not moving. That might just be a good idea, especially if it will relocate you nearer your family and other support systems. No, the mistake is changing things too quickly.

The need to do something urgently arises partly out of fear, but mostly out of plain, old-fashioned masochism. You want to hurt yourself or your departing spouse. If you're not careful you will hurt your children. Pain begets pain. It feeds off self-pity.

Drastic responses and impulsive decisions must be avoided at all costs. It can have a very unsettling effect on the children of divorce. Sudden changes greatly increase their already-high levels of anxiety and set up a highly unstable environment.

I speak here from personal experience. When my mother decided to separate from my father, a decision that I now see was made on the spur of the moment, she uprooted my younger brother and me and moved us all to another part of the town in which we lived. It may not seem so far, across town, but the impulsiveness of the move, the act of packing all our belongings into suitcases, leaving home and friends without even saying good-bye, and being forced to resettle into a temporary second home and go to a different school greatly increased the anxiety that my brother and I were experiencing. We were being called upon to make too many horrendous adjustments all within a matter of days. It was more than my young heart and mind could take!

It would have been enough just to have to cope with an announcement from my mother that she was going to get a divorce. I suppose she thought she was being protective of us, but it would have been less disturbing if she had simply sat down with us, explained what she wanted to do, and left us in our home for a while where everything in our young lives would have continued normally. This would also have allowed my mother and father to rationally discuss and plan a long-term strategy for dealing with us children.

Now I realize that there are other factors that prompt quick action. But all I am pleading for here is for some stability and a feeling of security for the children. The best antidote I know for a child facing the anxiety created by divorce is to experience ongoing stability.

If at all possible, the child's home environment and regular routine should be maintained. This makes it easier for the child to adjust first to the idea of the separation and divorce and then to prepare for its consequences.

Promises, Promises, Keep Your Promises

It is important for divorcing parents to remember another cardinal rule: *Don't make promises you can't keep.* Very often, parents try to ease their children's pain by making ridiculous promises.

Parents do this to alleviate their own guilt feelings. It helps them to feel better when they promise the sky to their children to make up for what they are doing.

Sometimes these promises are outrageous and there is no way they can be fulfilled. But guilt blinds parents' perceptions of reality. At other times these promises are realistic, though petty, but because they were offered as an atonement for guilt the parent conveniently forgets about them. If the child asks for the pay out and the parent has reneged, further tension between the parent and child ensues. It is better to refrain from trying to buy off your guilt!

One day, shortly after his divorce, Bob asked his oldest daughter, an attractive sixteen-year-old, "How would you like to go with me to Hawaii this summer?"

She was understandably thrilled. "Do you really mean it, Dad? Really?"

"Sure," replied Bob. But what he didn't say was that at that moment he knew he could not afford such a trip. He was heavily in debt. His credit cards were fully spent, and he was not due for any vacation leave for another year. Still, he made the promise, reiterated it, and set his daughter up for a major disappointment.

Why did he do it? To alleviate his guilt, obviously. He also knew that his daughter was about to discover he was having an affair with a work colleague and that this was what had precipitated his divorce. His intense feeling of guilt at that moment completely distorted reality for him. In a day or two he would come to his senses and hope his daughter wouldn't remember the promise. Chances are high that she will never forget and hold it against him for years to come. *Broken promises have long memories.*

Peter was not quite as generous when he asked his twelve-year-old son what he would like as a "special" present. Peter's divorce had just been finalized and he had this sudden urge to be kind to his son.

"Oh, Dad, I want an electric guitar."

"Sure. That's great. Let's go shopping for one over the weekend."

The weekend came and went. Little Peter had nagged, cajoled, cried, and threatened to run away. Finally he sulked his way to his bedroom where he hid so no one could find him. The problem is that no one came looking for him!

Dad was too busy that particular weekend. Maybe next weekend, if he could find the time!

But young Peter never got his guitar, or so he told me years later during his therapy. Father never really intended getting it for him. The promise was just a way of helping him to feel better. The fact that it made his son feel worse seemed to escape him.

These are just some of the stories I have heard of broken promises. Going places, doing fun things, buying toys; all promised by parents in moments of remorse or to get their children off their backs. Such unfulfilled promises teach children that they cannot trust anyone, especially those closest to them. It is far better never to promise anything than to fail to keep a promise. If you don't promise something but then give it, the child has a bonus, and bonuses are better than disappointments any day!

This is what is so wonderful about God. He never breaks His promises.

In fact he never promises anything he can't provide. First Kings 8:56 tells us, "there hath not failed one word of all his good promise . . ." Christian parent, this is our model. You could do no better than to imitate God in this matter. A trustworthy parent will produce trustworthy children, even if the family is divided.

Forcing Choices

Feeling rejected by an ex-spouse, some divorced parents feel insecure over their children, especially teenagers. They wonder "Does my child love me for who I am?" They even fear being rejected by a child just as the other partner did.

To resolve this inner conflict, parents may try to test a child's affection and allegiance by forcing the child to make a choice. "Do you love me or your father? Do you want to live with me or him?" Forced choices never lead to happy consequences.

"My mother asked me one day whether I wanted to stay with her or with my father," Betty explained to me. "'Why are you doing this to me,' I asked her. It's terrible when your parents do this to you. They get you to a point where you've got to choose between them. If you choose your mother, then you hurt your father's feelings. If you choose your father, then your mother is hurt. It's a no-win situation. So I just say the normal thing— girls should be with their mothers, and boys should be with their fathers."

The conflict created within the child by being forced to take sides can be very damaging to relationships with both parents. If it is repeated often or if the motive of the parent forcing the choice is to interfere with the child's relationship with the other parent, permanent emotional damage can be done.

Children are remarkably insightful and brutally just. They know most of the time what the parent is doing. They know if the parent is testing their love or using them to get at the other parent. Because they don't always feel the freedom to speak up against the other parent, they may internalize their conflicted feelings, pull away, and build up resentment that will later carry over to other relationships.

There is a host of subtle ways a parent can force choices on a child and make it appear that you are rejecting one or the other. "Are you coming with me to visit Grandma, or are you going with your father?" "Do you want to go to church with me or with your mother?" "What are you going to do during your summer vacation?"

Forced choices like these cause conflict for the child because no matter what they do, they lose. If a child chooses one parent, he or she is rejecting the other.

If a genuine choice has to be made, then the way the options are presented can make all the difference between a healthy response and a conflicted one. The choice should always be prefaced with a comment about the underlying dilemma of having to choose. Then give your child uncluttered freedom to make a free choice. Don't take it personally.

The following would be a healthy way of handling a vacation choice. "Honey, I know it is difficult to choose between me and your father, but I really need to know what you prefer. If you decide to go on vacation with your father I will understand perfectly why you make this choice. I won't be upset. I know it doesn't mean that you love me less."

The following simple steps can help a parent to avoid the pitfalls of genuine decision-making:

1. Admit to your child that having to choose between parents is a very painful task. This legitimizes your child's feelings and shows that you really understand the dilemma. Respect for you will increase at warp speed!

2. Reassure your child that he or she has total freedom to make his or her own choice, and that the child's choice will not affect your relationship.

3. Clearly present the options to the child, making sure that you do not communicate any bias.

4. Force yourself to accept the child's decision, whatever it is, without disappointment or resentment.

5. Tell your child you are satisfied with the decision, even if it is against you. This last step is important, because committing yourself with a positive statement like this can reinforce acceptance within yourself.

Commit yourself to the way you want to feel, and you will be surprised how quickly you actually come to feel this way.

Discovering Yourself

A more complete discussion of the many mistakes a parent can make in the postdivorce period could take up many books. The best help I can offer is summarized as follows: If you want to avoid making mistakes, work hard at understanding yourself. The better you know yourself, and particularly your motives, the healthier your children are going to be. Get professional help if necessary. It is well worth the trouble.

Humans can be remarkably naive, and they often act with little self-awareness. It is not that they are stupid or don't care about their children. They aren't and they do. But we all tend to say and do a lot of things without reflection or knowing why. Self-awareness doesn't come with our gene package! It is something we have to develop.

With greater self-awareness comes the ability to choose right actions and whether to act or not. A parent who knows why he or she feels a certain way can avoid saying or doing something damaging. By contrast, a parent who speaks or acts without self-understanding runs a high risk of making mistakes. It's like shooting a gun blindfolded; there's no way to tell where the bullet will end up.

Since for most people divorce is the result of accumulated failures, the postdivorce recovery period will only produce growth if the parties work at developing greater self-understanding. In other words, a divorced person must try to benefit from the mistakes of the past. And this can only happen if they take the time to examine the mistakes made in the previous marriage and try to extract from them everything they can about themselves. Divorce can be a school of hard knocks, but if you learn well, your life can be the better for it.

Some of us learn easily from our past mistakes. Others are slow learners—we need help. What can help? You need a sounding board, someone to talk to so as to clarify your thinking and test your ideas. For this reason I strongly recommend that every parent seek some form of counseling or therapy immediately following a divorce. This does not have to be in a professional setting, although this is often the easiest and most convenient way to do it. A competent pastoral counselor, a well-balanced and sensible close friend, or even an adult-support or divorce-recovery group at your local church can help tremendously.

At best, divorce is a difficult experience for a child to make sense of. Coping with the hurts and disappointments of a broken home, children need the support and help of two healthy, honest, and growing parents, even if they are headed in different directions. You owe it to your children to be the healthiest you can be, to be fully aware of what you are doing to yourself and to them. If the devastation of the divorce is to be turned around to become a positive experience, everyone must grow. What started out as a catastrophe can give way to a new closeness and depth of understanding that is often difficult to achieve even in intact families.

While I would not advocate that couples divorce just so they can all be the better for it, there is no reason why one should not strive for progress once divorce is inevitable.

CHAPTER 5

Your Child's Feelings

What does a child feel before, during, and after divorce? This basic question is very important, because the adjustments that must be made and the residual impact of the divorce on the child will largely be determined by these feelings. If you, as a divorced parent, can understand and accept these feelings and then find ways to help your child express these feelings, the detrimental effects of the divorce will be greatly reduced.

God is the great comforter. The spiritual healing he offers to us in Christ can have a remarkable effect on the physical and psychological consequences of any traumatic experience. As a parent you have a responsibility to help your child receive that comfort and healing. You are to be the channel for this comfort, but to do this effectively you must first come to understand what your child is feeling. This chapter is designed to help you do this.

Why We Run Away from Feelings

Unless you are a trained therapist you will most likely find the expression of painful feelings unpleasant and will want to avoid them. Men have more problems here than women, I'm sorry to say. So men may have to work a little harder at facing up to their feelings.

Because the feelings triggered by divorce, before, during, and after, are inherently intense it is quite natural that you will want to detour around them. Why? Because dealing with a child's hurt makes your hurt greater. It is bad enough trying to handle an adult's pain, but a child's pain cuts more deeply—ask any dentist or surgeon.

It is only human to want to avoid the pain of others. This is one of the reasons many people don't like hospitals. Their sympathetic feeling of the pain of those who are sick can be a problem. It is as if they take the pain of others upon themselves. This is what sympathy is all about, and it is a perfectly normal reaction. Those who enter the helping professions, such as psychiatry, clinical psychology, or medicine, are trained to overcome this sympathetic response. If they didn't they would never be able to give a shot, much less perform surgery. I remember in my youth trying to give a shot to our dog. I just could not bring myself to push the needle into his neck. I had to get the vet to do it.

But it is not only physical pain that gives us problems, but emotional pain as well. Helpers who are not trained easily succumb to burnout when they let emotional pain overwhelm them. This is why we train counselors to be empathic, not sympathetic. What is the difference? In empathy we try to enter into another's pain with understanding and not feeling. Sympathy enters into emotional pain with feeling, not understanding.

All this is to say that you must try to set aside your sympathy and try not to feel your child's pain. The harder you try to understand it, the more empathic you can be without your own feelings getting in the way. I know this isn't easy, but you have to try to keep your own feelings out of the way.

For the parent, the sympathetic response is often intensified by feelings of guilt. A parent may blame herself for what a child is experiencing, even though she may not be entirely to blame.

When a child shows distress, the first tendency of a parent is to either run away from the pain, for fear it will increase her own, or to try to stop the child from feeling the hurt so much. It is all done in subtle ways. For instance, the parent tries to shortcut the feelings by giving reassurance, or by telling the child, "Pull yourself together, it's not the end of the world."

Isn't it good to try and take away a child's painful feelings? Not really.

Feelings serve an important purpose in the healing process. Cutting off a child's feelings may stop this healing. The pain doesn't go away, it just slows down the harder work of adjustment by forcing the pain into the background. And because it is not out in the open, this buried pain can do a lot more damage than open and easily recognized pain.

When a child is prevented from expressing his or her feelings, especially over a loss, the very important process of grieving is short-circuited. Whatever else divorce means to a child, it is at least a significant loss of the family unit. Something dies, and that something must be grieved.

Much has been written in the past years about the grieving process and allowing the bereaved person to experience his emotional pain openly. The grieving process must run its course without being aborted or stifled. And this is equally true whether the loss is death or divorce.

In effect, what I am saying is that it is important that divorced parents not run away from their children's pain nor try to take away the pain that is necessary for grief to do its healing work. Your comfort level is not the issue here, but your child's healing is. And be assured that the comfort of God, ministered by his Spirit, is able to deal with the deepest of all human sorrows.

Comfort by Understanding

It is very clear from Scripture that not only are we to derive comfort from God, but we are also to comfort one another (see 1 Thessalonians 5:11). To be a comforter, one must first be an understander. The truth of this is borne out every day in the practice of a psychotherapist or counselor. People who jump in with words of advice or reassurance, without taking the time and trouble to first understand how another is feeling, are not effective as comforters. Even when your advice is filled with the wisdom of Solomon, it is not helpful by itself. I would say that a thousand words of advice are equivalent to just a few words of understanding. Why bother then with giving advice? Stick with trying to understand, and you will be a great comforter.

To really understand a child's feelings about divorce takes courage on the part of the parents—courage to move into another person's hurts without fearing that your own hurts will be increased and courage to listen and even to take the blame for the hurt without becoming defensive. And, paradoxically, parents who make this effort find that they themselves are also comforted by just trying to understand their child. I've seen this happen many times. I know it works.

Some years ago I worked with a family going through a divorce. Of the two children involved, the older boy, who was about fourteen years of age, had become deeply depressed. For many months, ever since he heard of the impending separation of his parents, his mood had been melancholic. He was sad, cried easily, and had withdrawn from all his friends. He stopped doing his homework, so his grades dropped. He spent all his spare time lying on the floor in his bedroom with headphones shutting out the world, listening to pop music. His father, who was the main instigator of the family breakup, saw how depressed his son was, and he too became severely depressed. He avoided his son, feeling guilty and utterly powerless to do anything to help.

"Can't you get my son out of his depression?" the father challenged me during a therapy session one day. "No, I can't," I replied, "but you can."

I then suggested that the father take his son on a fishing trip, hoping that this would give his son an opportunity to ventilate his feelings at his father.

"But won't it make him worse?" asked the father. (What he was really asking was, "Won't it make it worse for me?")

"Perhaps," I replied, "but we must take the risk."

The father agreed to try it, and that fishing trip was a healing experience for both father and son. They were able to really show each other how much they cared, and the father was able to develop a deep understanding of what his son was feeling. He did not defend or even try to explain his actions to his son; he just accepted his son's feelings for what they were.

While this did not save the marriage (and I must confess that I did pray that somehow the time with his son might turn things around), it did greatly reduce the emotional damage the boy may have suffered. It also ensured that the deep anger and resentment the boy was feeling toward his father would not harm their subsequent relationship. The father's extra effort at trying to understand his son brought a measure of healing to both of them.

What Does a Divorced Child Feel?

The feelings experienced by a child of divorce will change as time passes. As in the grieving process following the death of a loved one, there are clearly identifiable emotional stages through which children pass as they try to deal with the breakup of their family. The six stages are:

1. Fear and anxiety
2. Abandonment and rejection
3. Aloneness and sadness
4. Frustration and anger
5. Rejection and resentment, and
6. Reestablishment of trust.

These emotional stages are inevitable and normal. As a divorced parent, don't expect your child to miraculously bypass any of these stages. Pray rather that God will help him or her through them in a healthy way and that processing them will be a positive rather than a negative learning experience. Pray for your child to understand and accept these stages.

In the following pages we will look at each stage more closely and examine what you, as a parent, grandparent, or other relative, can do to facilitate adjustment to each stage.

Stage 1: Fear and Anxiety

The conflict between the parents just before a divorce can take many forms. In some homes the conflict is very visible; yelling, screaming, and fighting send very clear messages to the children that there is a problem. But children don't always see a divorce coming. Usually they deny the seriousness of conflict and engage in wishful thinking that all will work out in the long run.

At the other extreme some families use "silent" warfare for expressing conflict. There is no open fighting in front of the children, and no hint is given that anything is wrong. Children in these homes may come to hate the long periods of silence between the parents, but they too seldom expect that any serious family breakup is in the offing.

So it seems that no matter how open or hidden the conflict is, the final announcement of a separation and divorce is nearly always a surprise to the children. Their first emotional reaction is, therefore, one of panic, fear, and anxiety.

What causes these feelings? Suddenly a cavernous unknown is opened up in front of the child, and he or she is being pushed into it! Divorce is a threat to the child's very existence as he or she knows it, an unsettling of everything stable and certain in life. It is an emotional earthquake of the highest magnitude and shakes the very foundations of security.

It is natural that your child will feel fearful and anxious. Many of the classic signs of anxiety and fear may appear: sweating, restlessness, sleeplessness, nightmares, hyperventilation, tightness in the chest, gastrointestinal disturbances, and a variety of aches and pains. These symptoms are normal and should be accepted as such without overreacting or accusing the child of acting out. Give quiet reassurance and discuss your plans very clearly.

This last point is very important. We can all deal with what we know far better than with what we don't know or imagine. If a child is kept in the dark and not given the full facts about an impending divorce, he or she is likely to think up even worse possibilities. Imagination feeds anxiety, whereas facts create fears. But fears are easier to deal with than anxiety—and less damaging. In the long run, a child who knows exactly what is going on will be better equipped to handle his or her fears than one who is left to imagine the worst!

If a child is not yet old enough to understand or be given all the facts, or if there are other reasons for withholding information, it is especially important to provide physical reassurance. Spend time with the child. Show your love for him or her openly and frequently, for love is the great antidote for all fear and anxiety. Scripture tells us this clearly: "There is no fear in love; but perfect love casteth out fear" (1 John 4:18). What this verse really means is that we need not fear someone who loves us perfectly. But I think it goes beyond this; when we are loved perfectly, our fear of other things is also driven away.

Stage 2: Abandonment and Rejection

The fear and anxiety stage soon gives way to the next: feelings of abandonment and rejection. Even though deep down they may know it is not true, the children of divorce often feel that they are being abandoned and rejected by the spouse who leaves. "If my father really loved me, he wouldn't be leaving Mommy and me," one upset eight-year-old girl said to me once as she summed up her feelings.

Younger children tend to have these feelings more often than older children. They cannot always distinguish between the parents separating from each other and one of the parents separating from them.

Sometimes the parent who initiates the divorce is already involved with or soon becomes attached to a second potential spouse. If there are children in the second relationship, the feelings of rejection can become even greater, as the following story told by a twelve-year-old girl illustrates:

> My dad had just left home about three weeks before when he told me that he was going to marry this other lady. Then he began to show me pictures of her children—a boy and a girl just a little younger than me. I suppose he thought I would be happy about this—me being an only child and all that and feeling lonely a lot of times. Well, I began crying and shouting at him, right there in the restaurant. How could he do this to me? He never carried pictures of me in his wallet—or anything like that. It wasn't fair. He was leaving me for them.

Such feelings of abandonment can be significantly reduced if the departing parent would maintain a lot of contact with the child during the early stages of separation. This is usually the time when there is the most conflict between the parents and when there is likely to be little contact with the parent who leaves the home.

Parents need to call a truce at this time for the sake of the children.

This means that an extra effort must be made to stay in contact with all family members. You have to make an effort because it won't happen naturally! Telephone calls won't do it, either. What a child needs to overcome the feelings of abandonment is your actual, physical, warm presence.

In one situation where the mother had left the home, I arranged for her to return home every morning to be with her thirteen-year-old daughter for breakfast. The husband cooperated by leaving for work early enough to allow mother and daughter to be alone together for at least an hour before school. The mother could see to her daughter's clothes, arrange her schedule for the day, and take care of other motherly chores. We continued this arrangement for three months, and then slowly reduced the number of mornings they spent together as other contact times were substituted. I believe this greatly reduced any feelings of abandonment the daughter might have otherwise felt.

Stage 3: Aloneness and Sadness

Sooner or later a feeling of extreme aloneness and isolation sets in. Things seem quieter and children find that they have a lot more time on their hands than before. This is because regular family activities come to a halt. Mealtimes are no longer regular or family-together activities. Even the conflict that had filled the home atmosphere is gone and leaves a void. There is less fussing all around, and a loneliness sets in.

Some children are surprised to find that for the first time in their lives they feel a deep sadness. It is experienced as a pain in the stomach and a tightness in the chest. Hobbies are neglected. Pets are ignored. Energy is diminished. Eating is difficult. Most children lose interest in their schoolwork and friends. They just want to mope around. A depression has taken over.

In this stage children also begin to spend a lot of time thinking. In fact, this may very well be why they become sad. Some of this thinking is wishful daydreaming, fantasizing that parents will get together again and all problems will go away. Some of this thinking intensifies the sadness and precipitates crying spells.

These crying spells should not be discouraged, and parents should avoid making their children feel ashamed or embarrassed for their crying. Tears are an important and healthy outlet for the sadness children feel, and crying serves a very important physiological function in helping us overcome sadness and depression.

It is characteristic of our culture that we value the suppression of painful feelings, as I have discussed in chapter 1. A greater freedom to cry would probably be healthier for us both physically and psychologically. Jesus understood the importance of tears and even cried himself. I am reminded of the words of Jesus in Luke 6:21: "Blessed are ye that weep now: for ye shall laugh." What he is saying is simply this: Crying prepares the way for future joy!

Stage 4: Frustration and Anger

Following closely on the heels of sadness come feelings of frustration and anger. Children of divorce primarily want security and happiness. They also want to see a return to the way things were before the divorce. Because they cannot get what they want, their needs are blocked or neglected. When this happens, children experience a deep frustration out of which flow feelings of anger.

The relationship between anger and frustration is an interesting one. Anger as a response to frustration is primitively intended to help us overcome the blocking of some goal or desire. The child caught in divorce has many desires and goals blocked, so it is natural that there be anger. The problem is that the anger doesn't help to overcome the obstacles. Decisions are being made outside the realm of the child's influence, and no amount of anger on the child's part is going to change anything. The anger, therefore, becomes self-defeating and is often turned inward by the child, who may do something to hurt himself.

One angry fourteen-year-old boy in a family I was working with went to his father's workshop and cut himself quite deeply on the leg with a chisel. "I was just testing to see how sharp it was" was his excuse. But the depth of the cut and the deliberateness of the act clearly indicated that harming himself was the only way this boy could express his frustration and anger at his father. He was too small to take it out physically on his dad, so he took it out on himself.

Since anger constitutes a major adjustment problem for the children of divorce, I will be devoting a full chapter to a discussion of this topic. Suffice it for me to say at this point that feelings of anger must be accepted as a normal stage in the process of adjusting to the divorce. Don't react to these feelings with your own anger. You will only aggravate the situation and provoke more anger.

Children's anger should be received naturally with the assurance that the parent understands why they feel the way they do and does not blame them for their anger. A statement like "You have no right to be angry," doesn't help; children of divorce **do** have a right to be angry! What they need is help with how to handle their anger. "Tell me how angry you are" is an invitation to openness and a much better approach.

A parent who can receive the child's anger without defending or excusing himself or herself will be helping the healing process.

Stage 5: Rejection and Resentment

Frustration and anger now give way to rejection and resentment, especially toward the parents. The child is not necessarily over the feelings of anger, but for now anger takes a back seat.

Evidence of this stage is seen in the child who pulls away and places some emotional distance between himself or herself and the parent. Why does the child do this? There are two reasons, it provides some protection from further emotional pain, and it is a way of punishing the parent for what has happened.

Rejection can take the form of pouting, giving parents the silent treatment. The child doesn't come when called and won't respond when spoken to. When asked to do something, he or she resists or conveniently "forgets." Older children may become very critical and constantly condemn others, especially brothers and sisters. "That dress looks terrible," or "I don't like your hair" are common remarks from boys to their sisters and mothers.

Girls may use a different approach, making unfavorable comparisons to get at their fathers. "Mary's father always takes her away at weekends," or "Sarah says her father never shouts at her." Such criticisms help the girl to express deep-seated resentment.

All humans are prone to a phenomenon known as "reaction formation," and it is helpful if parents understand it. When we hate someone but feel guilty and can't express it, we change the hate into love, which is more acceptable. In other words, we form a reaction to something we don't like in ourselves by converting it into the exact opposite. The problem is that the love that replaces the hate may only be superficial. It has an unreal feeling about it. But it is sometimes the only way we can deal with our unacceptable hate.

Reaction formation also works the other way around. When we desperately want to be loved but fear that we may be rejected, we turn our longing for love around and begin to show hate.

Both these reactions are quite common in the children of divorce. We hate a parent but can't face up to this hatred, so we make believe that we love. Alternatively, we want to be loved during the time of upheaval in the family but fear rejection, so we turn our love to hate.

This often happens when children go through the rejection and resentment stage. They push their parents away when they really want to be held, or they say hateful things when they want the parents to be loving. It is the child's way of protecting itself from being rejected.

A wise parent will see this behavior for what it is: a desperate attempt to gain love. Don't be put off by the hateful reactions.

One nine-year-old girl whose mother had left her husband engaged in this rejecting behavior. She would go into her mother's bedroom and let go with a barrage of "I hate you, I hate you" statements. When the mother tried to reason with her, the daughter would leave the room. The mother became confused about her daughter's feelings. "If she hates me this much now, what will she feel when she is grown up?"

I reassured the mother and explained what "reaction formation" was all about. "Ignore the verbal statements and see the behavior as a desperate cry for your love and reassurance," I told her. "Just take her in your arms and hold her. If she fights and wants to pull away, keep holding her gently," was my advice.

The mother followed my suggestion. The child fought, screamed, and kicked, but the mother held her firmly and close to her, repeating the words, "I love you, Jeannie. I love you, Jeannie." Slowly the anger subsided and the child nestled into her mother's arms. She lay there passively at first, but later began to return her mother's embrace. Mom had learned an important lesson: Children don't always mean what they say, and they often say the opposite of what they mean.

Stage 6: The Reestablishment of Trust

The final stage, in which trust is reestablished, is a very freeing one. When it comes, it is as if a fresh breeze has begun to blow in an otherwise hot and stuffy room. How long does it take from the beginning of a divorce until the final stage is reached? It varies from situation to situation.

Many factors are involved. Recovery time depends on the nature of the marital conflict, on the age and personality of the child, on how each parent has managed the subsequent problems, and on the healthiness of how the parents have related to one another. It could take a few months or it may take a few years—sometimes it takes many years.

What can a parent do to make sure that the child's feelings return to normal as soon as possible? Here are some simple rules that should speed up the process considerably:

Try not to be preoccupied with your own feelings.

It is so easy, during the difficult time of the separation and divorce, to be insensitive to the feelings of your children. Make time for their feelings. Set aside a period of the day or early evening when you can give attention to what they want to tell you. This will help you keep your own feelings in proper perspective and will give your children a chance to understand theirs.

Allow time for healing.

Divorce is not the time to be impulsive or to expect quick remedies. Your child needs time for important processing, so you will need to be patient. Ask God to increase your patience and understanding of what must take place before full healing can be expected. If this is a problem for you, then seek help from a pastoral counselor or other professional.

Maintain a stable home environment.

Whenever possible, keep your children in their regular home, going about their regular business, attending their regular school, and playing with their regular friends. The less you change things the better. They have enough to adjust to as it is! Changes can be made at a later stage when everything else has stabilized.

Don't become defensive.

Because you will no doubt be feeling very guilty about the divorce, you will have a strong need to defend yourself. This defensiveness invariably leads to more conflict. In particular, avoid attacking your ex-spouse for his or her actions. Doing so creates tension for your children, who have to keep the peace with both parents and should not be forced to take sides. Trust your child's sense of justice. He knows better than you who is to blame and how much blame should be apportioned to each parent. Because you are a hurt party, you cannot be fair in your judgments. Leave these to God who knows all things.

CHAPTER 6

What Children Learn from Divorce

Whatever else divorce is for a child, it is at least a major learning experience. It is a brutal school with many hard knocks.

And it isn't a single, time-limited, short-lived learning experience either. It is an ongoing issue with which children must grapple, often for years. This one life-event can have far-reaching consequences on the subsequent development of a child's personality, attitudes, behaviors, and abilities. How the child adjusts to later life will be heavily influenced by what she learns from the divorce.

Most experts agree that it takes between three and four years for a child to pull himself together again and pick up where the divorce leaves off. For an eight-year-old, this represents about a third of his or her life!

Throughout this period a divorced parent's behavior, feelings, and attitudes will be fully tested and on full display. His or her true nature will be drawn out for all to observe, both inside and outside the family. Divorce raises your true colors to the top of the mast.

This testing would not be all that serious if a parent's behavior did not affect others. Unfortunately, divorce is not a "victimless" life-experience. Parents cannot claim that they are the only ones affected by it, because they're not.

Since "modeling" is one of the major ways in which children learn right behavior, feelings, and attitudes, the modeling that parents do before, during, and after divorce can have a major impact on what children learn.

But what is modeling? It is the process by which one person learns by imitating or copying the behavior of another. It is a very important process in the development of a child's personality.

Modeling explains why our behavior so often closely resembles that of our parents. I'll never forget the day, as a teenager, that I looked in the mirror and saw my father's expression on my face. I panicked! It was quite eerie to see the resemblance, not just in appearance, but in behavior. Without realizing it, we copy those close to us from the time we are very small—the way they speak, walk, act, respond, and emote all rubs off on us. Fortunately, some of what we pick up through modeling is good. But a lot of it is of doubtful value.

Whether we like the idea or not, the behavior and feelings brought out by the conflicts surrounding a family breakup provide important grist for the children's learning mill. To illustrate this let me tell you of a woman who once came to see me for therapy. Don't think of her story as uncommon; it is more common than you realize.

Mary is the mother of a handsome seven-year-old son. To outsiders she appeared to be happily married to a young business executive who provided her with a very comfortable living. Outwardly, this family appeared happy and contented. But this only goes to show how deceptive appearances can be. Beneath the surface life was a living hell for Mary.

When Mary first consulted me she had great difficulty admitting what her problem was. For several sessions she beat around the bush. Finally it came out. She would hit her son for the most trivial of reasons. She wasn't a full-blown abuser, but her need to lash out was far in excess of what would be considered reasonable punishment for any misdeed.

"Am I a child beater?" she kept asking me.

She also had a tendency to lash out physically with her husband whenever he angered her. "I have to leave the house when Mary gets mad," he told me later, "because once she starts hitting on me there is no stopping her."

Where and when did Mary learn to use physical means for resolving conflicts? As I explored her past the reason become obvious—this was the way Mary's mother had behaved in her unhappy marriage to an alcoholic. From an early age, her mother had modeled physical aggression for Mary. How could she not have learned to behave this way?

Often coming home late at night in a drunken stupor, Mary's father would so frustrate her mother that she would physically lash out at him. And then it took a turn for the worse. "Come and hit your father," she would say to Mary. "He's a terrible man. Look what he's doing to us."

At first Mary refused. Turning, she would run out of the room. But one day her father retaliated and hit her mother. This was more than Mary could take, so she lashed out in childish rage, beating her fists on her father's chest in imitation of her mother and shouting, "Don't hit my mommy like that!"

Gradually, over those early years, Mary learned to deal with frustration by physically attacking the object causing the frustration. Now this behavior was coming out in her own marriage which, of course, bore no resemblance to that of her parents. Her husband wasn't an alcoholic. He was a gentle, kind man. But as in every marriage there come times when conflict arises. Mary had learned only one way to resolve conflict, and that was to lash out.

She was the victim of unintentional modeling. The long therapeutic road ahead was used to retrain Mary and teach her how to resolve frustration in healthier ways. Physical violence is not a healthy way to express anger under any condition, but unfortunately, divorce can sometimes only teach this solution.

Behaviors That Divorce Teaches Your Children

Because conflict and divorce are bosom buddies, the behaviors likely to be taught children during divorce are all variations of the anger and hostility theme. Divorce never teaches children how to be more loving or kind! It only has one subject in its curriculum, hate and hostility.

All this is to say that in those rare instances where a marital breakup involves little overt conflict, the atmosphere is usually healthier. This is only true if passive and indirect ways of showing anger are not being used to cover up a deeper hostility. Just because there is a lot of silence between a husband and wife doesn't mean there is no conflict. Just because couples keep their distance from each other doesn't mean they live in Utopia. Cover-up behaviors such as distancing, pouting, and silence are also unhealthy ways for handling conflict. Although, I must say that if I were to choose between the two evils of open warfare versus the cold war, I would prefer it if parents used the cold war method. It is just a little less damaging to children. Not much, but enough to make a difference.

What behaviors is your child most likely to learn from divorce? Allow me to mention a few to help you as a parent guard against modeling a detrimental behavior:

Hate

"It takes a lot more to hate somebody than it does to love them." These words were spoken to me by a thirteen-year-old girl, the victim of a recent divorce. She was describing her feelings for her parents.

Divorcing parents often give their children very effective lessons in the energy-draining art of hate. They openly display their hatred for each other on every occasion. Through callous disregard for what they say and do they teach their children not only how to hate, but the fact that hating pays dividends. Hating punishes people. Hate is a weapon more devastating than the sharpest sword or the most powerful bullet. It leaves permanent scars. When you've learned how to use hate, you don't need any other weapon. It does all the damage you want to inflict on anyone.

Distrust

Divorced kids learn that you cannot trust anyone, especially those who claim to love you the most. Simon is twelve. Listen as he explains, "We see my dad every second weekend. When he picks up my younger brother and me, the first thing he tells us is, 'Don't say anything to your mother about my new apartment and things. It only upsets her.' As soon as we get home in the evening, Mom asks us lots and lots of questions about where we went and what went on, about Dad's apartment, who was there, and what did they say. I try not to tell her anything, but later she gets me to say something. I tell her, 'Please Mom, don't tell Dad I told you anything!' Five minutes later I hear her shouting at my dad on the telephone about what I had said. I just know Dad's going to be angry at me next time. He won't trust me, but it's not my fault."

Later in life, Simon may generalize distrust of his parents to many other people. He will always be afraid to be open and honest for fear that his honesty will come back to punish him.

Sneakiness

Every divorced child I have ever met hates one aspect of what their parents want them to do more than any other—being called on to spy.

A major task for the children of divorce is learning to remain "friends" with both parents. And it's not easy when each parent is trying to get the children on his or her side. Children often end up being unwilling double agents. And as with every spy story I have ever read, double agents always get the shaft!

Before her parents' divorce, one fourteen-year-old girl was recruited by her mother to check her father's car regularly for evidence of "another woman." "Search behind the seats, in the glove compartment, and in the trunk," she was instructed. Like so many others in her position, this little girl came to hate and despise herself for being so sneaky, especially when her parents claimed to be Christians and talked about love and trust with their neighbors but never practiced it on themselves. This young girl will be lucky if she doesn't become sneaky and hypocritical herself.

Lying

"If you are going to survive, you have got to learn how to lie," explained one adolescent to me when describing the life he lived between two homes and two sets of parents. I felt like he was educating me!

"They lie to me all the time," he continued. "They used to lie about where they were going and what they were doing before the divorce. I knew my father was having an affair and so was my mother. When I called them on it, they got very angry and said I didn't understand about these things and that one day I would be a grownup and it would all be clear. Now, when I go where I can get some fun and they ask me where I've been, I lie just like they do!" Have you any idea how difficult it is to convince a teenager like this that lying doesn't pay?

These are just a few of the behaviors that divorce teaches if you are not careful as parents to watch your own behavior. They are all negative and destructive lessons. I am sure some readers are asking by now, "Are there no positive lessons that a child can learn from divorce?"

There certainly are, but before I list them let me say that it takes a lot more effort and deliberate planning on the part of parents to teach them. Negative behaviors are like weeds: They grow without nurture and flourish when neglected. As a child I once tried to grow weeds. I had dug up a patch of our garden and declared it mine. I promptly transplanted a dozen weeds, not knowing the real difference between them and flowers. I watered them every day. And they all died! Weeds, like bad behaviors, don't like attention. Pretty flowers, like good behaviors, are the opposite and thrive on attention. Nurturing them will help them to grow.

Given the sinful and selfish nature of human existence, people learn the negative and destructive lessons of life without any effort. The positive and healthy aspects require a little more determination if they are going to be learned.

Here are some of the good things to be learned from divorce if they are carefully cultivated by loving parents (even if they are divorcing):

Love and kindness in response to hate

There is really no reason why parents who are divorcing need to engage in the hostile behaviors they typically do. Admittedly, divorce makes more enemies than any other relationship, and it is a most unfortunate end to a union that was designed to be a bit of heaven. But usually one partner does not want the marriage to end. If both partners have agreed to divorce, then usually there is a reason for the one to feel rejected by unfaithfulness or betrayal.

But no matter what the reason, should this be the cause of bitter, open warfare? Why is it so difficult to lay aside the antipathy provoked by divorce, if only for the child's sake? This is really only a rhetorical question. I'm not naive, and I know that calling a truce is just about impossible in the early stages of divorce, but I still think we should strive to achieve it.

When parents set aside their personal grievances for the sake of their children, all heaven's angels surely must sing the "Hallelujah" Chorus. If that isn't worth some attention in heaven, then what is?

Please note, however, that I am not speaking here of love as a feeling but as behavior. If we are to love our enemies, then surely that also includes a former spouse. The description of love given in 1 Corinthians 13 has nothing to do with feelings. It is a prescription for how we should behave, even to those who might "despitefully use us."

Forgiveness and restoration for resentment

While hate and resentment might be innate to humans, forgiveness is not. *It is something we learn.* Did you get that?

A child who is not shown how to forgive grows up not knowing how to forgive. In divorce, actions speak louder than words. A parent's every movement, attitude, and reaction will be closely observed by the children. For this reason, it is important for divorced or divorcing parents to do everything possible, even to the point of seeking outside professional help, to heal their resentment and practice forgiveness over and over again.

Modeling forgiveness at a time when parents are hurting the most surely has to be the most effective way for them to teach it.

Patience and endurance in the face of impulsive urges

Divorce is a time when decisions are made impulsively and when tolerance for frustration is at its lowest. One is operating on a reserve tank already, so where can one find any extra reserves for patience? I know of only one place—next to the heart of God.

It takes effort to overcome the frightening insecurities provoked by divorce. The tendency is strong to abandon hope. It is so much easier just to throw in the towel and give up.

It is at times such as these that one has to reach beyond oneself and take God's hand to strengthen your own feeble hand. Parents can teach a powerful lesson about how to trust God to give patience and endurance. Their children will never forget such a lesson.

Improving Your Child's Resiliency

In an earlier chapter I pointed out that children differ in their ability to bounce back after a traumatic experience. Psychologists refer to this as "resilience." People who are successful in later life have invariably learned how to be resilient in their earlier life.

How can you as a divorced parent improve your child's resiliency? Obviously, whatever you can do to improve your child's ability to bounce back during this difficult time will have benefits later. Resiliency learned now will carry over into other areas of life.

Even a divorce, therefore, can be turned into a force for growth. Here are some suggestions for helping this to happen:

Don't be afraid to be honest with your child.

A child can cope much better with fears that are based on truth than with fears fed by imagination.

This is true because of the way we are made. Any threat to our well-being creates a reaction in our bodies that prepares us to deal with it as an emergency. In the case of reality-based fears, there is a limit to the threat. By contrast, fears based on imagination know no limits. They feed anxiety or worry and often turn little problems into big ones. Anxiety and worry are much more damaging to both our mental and physical health than real fears.

Many of the so-called psychosomatic disorders have their origin in anxiety and worry, not reality-based fears. Seldom do we develop these strange conditions when we face a real problem.

There are many reasons why parents fear being honest with their children. One is that they themselves fear the truth. Another is that they fear the way their children will react, expecting the worst. But the real problem with not being honest is that there is bound to be a day of reckoning sooner or later. Parents can only postpone the truth, they never change it! Their children will find out the truth sooner or later, and then they are likely to be more devastated by the implied lack of trust shown by their parents than by the pain parents tried to protect them from.

Of course, being honest doesn't mean being insensitive. Timing is also important. A parent shouldn't just dump all the truth on the child at once. In general, be guided by the principle that your child should not experience any unpleasant surprises or sudden revelations. Answer questions put to you honestly and don't evade the truth unless you have very good reasons for doing so.

Communicate trust to your child.

Children want to be trusted. They want to be given responsibility, and they often respond with surprising maturity when they have been respected. Children want to feel that their parents believe in them.

I have yet to find a child who does not respond to trust. Often the most recalcitrant and disobedient of children can be turned around by convincing them that they are trustworthy. It's a risk, I know, but many therapeutic agencies dealing with juvenile delinquents are successful in their treatment because they use this principle. So don't be afraid to show trust and give responsibility. Allow your child to make important decisions or take on increased duties. He or she will thrive on this implied trustworthiness.

Give liberal explanations but not defensive excuses.

Because parents often feel guilty about what they have done to their children, they tend to become excessively defensive and try to explain all their actions away. This doesn't help. What children need are rational, nondefensive, clear explanations. "Just give me the facts, Mom," said one twelve-year-old boy. "I'll decide whether or not Dad is wrong." And he was right! His mother was too preoccupied defending herself, and her son could see through the ploy and called her on it. Smart kid!

Why are explanations better than defensive excuses? Defenses are too emotionally charged. The facts become distorted and therefore create further confusion in the child's mind. Explanations should just stay with the facts. They should be as free of emotional bias as possible. Objective explanations will encourage a child to come out of his or her corner and courageously face reality.

Allow time for processing.

The human brain takes time to process things and can only cope with one predicament at a time. When children are confronted with a major change in their life's status as a result of divorce, they need time to process the change. The more extensive the change, the more time they need for processing it.

Parents often make the mistake of being too eager for their children to "get over" the divorce. Many forget that while they have had plenty of time to do their processing before they announced the divorce, the children have not had the same amount of time to adjust. Not allowing time for processing is likely to lead to impatience and increased tension and will probably disturb the relationship between parents and children. When children are given sufficient time to process their changed status they bounce back much more quickly.

Give freedom of choice.

One of the unfortunate by-products of divorce is that children lose their freedom of choice. They don't get to decide what happens to them, others do. For very young children this is not as critical as it is for older children and teenagers who often feel violated because they don't have any say in the decisions that are made about them.

While a child doesn't have the freedom to choose the divorce, there are many other areas where they can be given decision-making responsibility and a measure of control over their lives.

For example, whom should they live with after the divorce? What visiting rights should be allowed? Does the family move to another home? Who gets to keep the dog? Should they change schools? Children should be given an opportunity to choose. Teenagers, especially, should be allowed to influence these important decisions and should always be consulted *before* the final choices are made. If they are party to the decision-making process, they will not only feel better about the decision, but they will cooperate more fully on whatever the outcome is.

Build the child's security.

A child's resiliency is greatest when he or she can bounce back into a stable and secure environment. My grandchildren recently acquired a trampoline. It is easy to jump high when you know you will land safely on the tarp. Trouble starts when you miss and fall off the edge!

This is why I advocate that parents change as little as is absolutely necessary of the child's environment, home, school, and neighborhood during and immediately after a divorce. The more a child's world is changed, the greater the required adjustments will be, and the greater the adjustments demanded, the more likely it is that the child will not succeed in making them.

Dealing with Resiliency Failure

When a child is failing to adjust to the changes demanded of him or her, a number of warning signs can be recognized. These will be the focus of the chapters to follow. At this point let me just say that if you are not satisfied with how your child is adjusting, seek help. First, get as much information as you can. Ask the child's teacher for a report on how he or she is doing at school, and ask the other siblings how they see their brother or sister coping with the stress of change. Your minister or family physician can refer you to a specialist who can help guide you as you help your child. Follow the principle that the sooner you nip a problem in the bud, the less likely it will become a permanent problem.

Whatever the specific problem you may have to deal with, bear in mind that a divorced child usually has three questions on his or her mind:

+ When will my daddy (or mommy) come home?
+ When will my parents get back together again?
+ Will they ever get divorced again?

Satisfactory answers cannot always be given to these vexing questions. For many children there is no other way but to go forward, accepting what has happened and learning how to live with their new life-circumstances.

This year there will be over one million children asking these questions and discovering that divorce is not a bad dream that goes away when you wake up. Only last night I had a bad dream about one of my grandchildren. The relief I felt when I woke up and found it was only a dream is inexpressible. Imagine children who keep waiting to wake up!

To ensure that a child's processes of biological, social, and emotional growth continue in a normal and healthy way, it is important that parents be alert to the signs of trouble and have the courage to take corrective action before any serious harm is done. That will be my focus as we continue to examine the effects of divorce on children.

CHAPTER 7

Anxiety and the Divorced Child

It was late one night when I received an urgent phone call from a former patient. I had seen her over a period of four months concerning a problem with her marriage. I guessed, therefore, that she was calling for help because of trouble again with her husband. Her predicament was not conflict and fighting but indifference; her husband had lost interest in her some time ago, and she had been forced to build an independent life for herself.

But the call wasn't directly about her husband. "My daughter is in a terrible state," she explained over the telephone. "I don't know what is happening to her. She needs help."

She went on to update me on her life. She had recently decided to separate from her husband but had waited until a week ago to share her intentions with her two daughters. One was away at college, but the other, the subject of the telephone conversation, was still at home, a senior in high school. Two days previously, while preparing a project report for school, the younger daughter had begun sweating profusely. She complained of pains in her chest and difficulty in breathing. Most frightening of all, she had begun to feel the most intense feelings of impending doom. She was overcome by an intense fear and started crying so hysterically that her mother had to rush her to the emergency room.

After a day of diagnostic testing the message the mother got from the doctor was: "There is nothing physically wrong with your daughter. She is experiencing a severe anxiety attack with hyperventilation." In other words, the daughter's anxiety was out of control and she needed to see a psychologist or psychiatrist. So she called me.

I agreed to see the daughter the next morning. She was still experiencing quite a bit of panic and was unable to tell me clearly why she was anxious. This is not unusual. Panic attack sufferers can't always pinpoint the source of their anxiety.

Only after much prompting did she admit that her mother's intention to separate from her father was causing her some apprehension. The truth is that she was deathly afraid of what was happening and trying her best to deny that it was a big deal. The problem is that the body can recognize a lie!

Severe anxiety reactions before, during, or after a marriage annulment are quite common in the children of divorce. The reactions can vary from mild to dramatic. I think it is safe to assume that every divorce provokes some anxiety in the children. Some don't show it so openly.

For some, anxiety provokes a regression to an earlier pattern of childish behavior. Bedwetting, after a child has been potty trained, is an example of such regression. For others, the anxiety may be the beginning of a nervous habit such as nail-biting or nervous tics. Many adults who bite their nails can trace the habit's origin to an episode of early life anxiety.

What Is Anxiety?

Everyone is capable of experiencing anxiety. The system that causes anxiety is normal and embedded in the marvelous brain that God has given us.

But what triggers this anxiety system? The trigger is part of the fear-response mechanism that is also designed into us as part of an elaborate system of defense. If we did not experience fear, we would not live beyond the first few years of life. We would be destroyed by our carelessness and lack of danger awareness. Our fear of fire, for example, keeps us from getting burned.

Anxiety is, in essence, a distorted form of fear. But not everyone recognizes or can accurately label the form of fear that we call anxiety. Some experience it only in its mildest form, even when confronted with a major catastrophe, while others feel it intensely, even under very mild threats. Take, for example, the way some people react to giving a speech. There is no real danger. Listeners don't harm you. Yet we sometimes react with severe anxiety as if our very lives were threatened.

Anxiety, then, is a loose term for an imprecise feeling of uneasiness or fear. It is more than worrying and may be accompanied by many physical symptoms.

Occasional feelings of anxiety have no long-term damaging effects. Going to the dentist doesn't scar you for life! But when anxiety persists over a prolonged period or when it is very intense, it can cause many chronic illnesses. A child is not well equipped yet to handle insecurity, threats of abandonment, financial and emotional deprivation, and the loss of a significant person such as a parent. Yet this is what every child must experience in divorce. And out of this experience comes anxiety of varying intensity which, if not attended to, can launch a child down Neurosis Lane.

How can the damaging effects of anxiety be avoided? By recognizing its early signs and taking a few basic steps to alleviate it.

How Divorce Produces Anxiety

There are many ways in which divorce can generate anxiety, as well as fear, in children. I will discuss a few so that you may get a sense of where the danger lies for your child:

Feelings of abandonment

I pointed out earlier that the very first reaction of every child to being told of an impending divorce is one of anxiety. The very young child, who cannot yet understand the subtleties of adult relationships, feels that the parent leaving the home has abandoned him or her. And there is a lot of evidence to show that abandonment is exactly what happens. Despite the best intentions in the world, a departing father is likely to be an absent father. Forty percent of kids in female-headed homes haven't seen their fathers in at least a year! There is a sort of paternal amnesia that takes over.

An absent parent creates an exaggerated need for that parent, and the anxiety increases when this need is not met.

The custodial parent, usually a mother, can't always understand the need for the absent parent. "How can she keep crying for her father?" one distraught mother complained to me once. "She's always ignored him before. Now suddenly he is everything to her." Such reversals of affection can cause the home parent to feel rejected or unappreciated by the child.

While this is all very painful to the parent, the more serious problem is that the child may actually believe he or she *has* been abandoned. Many children cry out hysterically, "Why has Daddy left me?" Sometimes this feeling leads the child to believe that he is the cause of the parent's departure. Such guilt feelings accelerate the general level of anxiety.

Loss of a stable environment

Closely related to feelings of abandonment as a generator of anxiety is the trauma of losing a stable environment. Children need a steady, unchanging, and loving home base if they are going to be free of anxiety. Neurotic anxiety, that form of anxiety that is irrational and unfounded, is most likely to develop in persons who do not have a stable home environment. Divorce, of all life's experiences, has the greatest potential to unsettle this environment.

Separation anxiety

Some psychologists see divorce as a major threat to a child because it creates "separation anxiety," a very distinctive form of anxiety found in divorced children.

When a child is simultaneously exposed to stress and detachment from a parent, his or her capacity to respond to later separation from significant others can be permanently damaged. As an adult such a person finds it intolerable when separated from a loved one, even temporarily.

Embarrassment and a sense of shame

Despite the fact that divorce has become commonplace, and children know they are not alone in it, the feeling of being stigmatized and embarrassed is still a very powerful generator of anxiety. When my parents split, divorce was just beginning to be socially acceptable. Even though my friends were understanding, and I knew that some of them were also the products of broken homes, I still felt intense embarrassment and shame.

At school functions I would often be asked to explain the absence of my father. Perhaps it was a school play or a sporting event. I would be asked, "How come your mother is here but not your father?" Insensitive teachers, malicious classmates, and unsuspecting strangers became my enemies; I was constantly on guard against such embarrassing questions.

Finally I decided that it would be better if my mother did not come to school events. That way my father's absence would be less conspicuous.

When I attracted my first girlfriend, I was not quite prepared for her parents' reaction to the discovery that my parents were divorced. I was barely fourteen at the time and infatuated with a classmate. It was my first experience of "love." She was my ideal! She was also the class idol. It would be a feather in my popularity cap if I could become her "special" boyfriend.

On that first visit to her home I tried to be on my best behavior. I began to fantasize about our future. Wouldn't it be perfect if we could marry one day? Then I sat up with a start! What would she think when she finds out my parents were divorced? She knew little about my family. I knew she had happy parents. What would they think of me when they found out? So I carefully avoided any reference to my family.

I went home and became depressed. Because of my exaggerated fears of her reaction I decided to pull away rather than risk rejection. It would be many years before I again let myself risk the intimacy of a girlfriend relationship. My shame posed a significant obstacle to my future happiness.

But is such a reaction confined to an earlier era? Recent events have convinced me that this reaction is just as common today as it was then. Many boys feel this shame, especially if they grow up in a Christian environment. One young man I know nearly called off his marriage recently when his parents decided to divorce. The reason? The girl's parents told her that "children from divorced homes divorce more easily than others." I tried to explain that such an idea was not only untrue but didn't quite apply to him since he was not a child when his parents called it quits.

Within our Christian circles there is still a stigma attached to divorce that can cause shame, and therefore anxiety, in children.

Fear of the unknown

Perhaps the greatest anxiety generator of all is the fear of the unknown. The very young child is oblivious to what is happening. Older teenagers have begun to develop the resources needed to fend for themselves. But in-between there are children who neither know what to expect nor have the resources to cope with uncertainty. For them anxiety can go through the roof.

Divorce opens up a great unknown. It is ominous and dangerous, and a child is invited, no, forced to plunge into its unknown depths. What will happen to me? Will we be poor? Will Daddy give us a new mommy? Who will she be? Fairy-tale stepmothers are always wicked! Will Mommy give us a new daddy? Will he be cruel? Do we have to move? Where will we stay? What school will I go to? These are the questions that flood the mind of a younger child, and they create intense feelings of anxiety.

How Anxiety Shows Itself in Childhood

How can a parent know when a child is reacting with an unusually high level of anxiety? There are a number of important clues, but before discussing these let me emphasize that some anxiety (it is more likely to be mixed with fear) is normal and necessary to your child's healthy development. So don't be concerned about mild anxious reactions. Excessive anxiety, however, should receive prompt parental action. If not, the anxiety will remain a problem for a long time. Let me illustrate.

Jimmy, aged seven and an only child, had a severe anxiety reaction when his parents decided to divorce. His anxiety showed itself almost immediately in a number of ways, but his parents were too preoccupied with their own problems to give him the attention he needed. Subsequently, Jimmy's mother decided she couldn't handle him and asked his grandmother to take care of him for a while.

"He is acting up," she told Jimmy's grandmother. "I don't know why he is being so difficult. Just let me get over my problems and I'll be able to cope again."

Poor Jimmy now had to contend with a double trauma. Not only had his father left home, but now he felt abandoned by his mother as well. His mother finally reestablished their home five weeks later, but by then Jimmy had become attached to his grandmother and didn't trust his mother. Wrenching him away from her was another traumatic blow.

The lack of attention to Jimmy's anxiety state slowly caused it to become a generalized reaction to all of his life. He became an excessive worrier, fearful of many situations. As a young adult he now spends an inordinate amount of time avoiding situations that bother him. His thinking is totally dominated by anxious fears. And the saddest fact of all is that his problem could have been avoided with early help.

Divorcing parents owe it to their children to avoid creating such neurotic patterns. The child who is helped by sensitive and nurturing parents, even though they are divorced, has a better chance for healthy adulthood than even a child from an intact but unhappy home.

The Symptoms of Childhood Anxiety

The symptoms of childhood anxiety can be divided into three categories: physical, psychological, and social. I will discuss each in turn and through illustration try to help you determine whether or not your child has a problem that needs help.

Physical symptoms

Severe or prolonged anxiety produces a disturbance of almost every system of the body. Children, like adults, sometimes have a weakness where they most readily show their anxiety. Some feel it as discomfort in the stomach or intestinal system, others in the cardiovascular system. Still others have problems with their respiratory system. Occasionally a child may show anxiety through symptoms involving more than one of these systems.

The most common physical reaction is in the gastrointestinal tract. Stomachaches, nausea, vomiting, or diarrhea can occur either continuously or sporadically. Often the child will only display these symptoms during very stressful situations, such as when separating after a parental visit, returning to school after a vacation, or moving to another home.

Headaches are the next most common physical reaction to stress. Parents should be alert, however, to children who exaggerate the severity of their pain to get sympathy and attention.

The most common type of headache is of the tension variety, but occasionally a true migraine headache may be triggered by stress in a child's life. Migraine headaches are quite common among girls, especially after they have reached puberty. The migraine attack occurs shortly before the onset of menstruation and ceases before it is over. Differentiating tension headaches from migraine headaches is important because they are treated differently. Consult a physician if necessary.

Whatever the type of headache, the underlying cause, anxiety and tension, must be addressed. Both parents can help by providing reassurance, love, and understanding.

Cardiovascular symptoms are rare in younger children but can occur in older children, especially teenagers. Complaints of heart palpitations, cold hands and feet, chest pains, dizziness, and fainting spells are the most common anxiety reactions here. The child may have a hyperventilation attack in which overbreathing triggers a host of strange sensations in the body.

Respiratory problems can occur at all ages. Increased frequency of asthmatic discomfort or allergy attacks, difficulty in breathing, tightness in the chest, and a greater susceptibility to chest infections can all be connected with anxiety.

Physical habits such as nail-biting, bedwetting, and thumb-sucking may either begin during a period of increased anxiety or, if these tendencies already exist, intensify. Sleep may become disturbed, and the child may have more nightmares than usual. Some children wake up frightened and want to come to the parent's bedroom seeking comfort and security. They may refuse to sleep by themselves and act up when bedtime arrives. Firm, loving boundaries here will help the child to feel secure.

Psychological symptoms

Increased irritability and a tendency to quarrel with other siblings and friends are the most common psychological symptoms of anxiety. A child's tolerance for frustration, delays, and disappointments may drop dramatically; when they ask for something, they want it immediately. Temper tantrums may increase in frequency and be used by the child as an outlet for tension and hostility.

Children who experience extreme anxiety reactions also tend to show disturbances in their normal activities. They become clingy and shadow their mother or father everywhere. These symptoms are directly related to the anxiety triggered by separation from a parent or the threat of further separation. They want to stay close to the remaining parent at all times.

Other anxiety symptoms include a morbid fear of certain toys and objects and a preoccupation with the fear that an accident or illness will befall their parents or themselves. Children worry about getting lost and not being reunited with their parents. Concern about dying may also emerge.

Social symptoms

The first reaction a child may have when experiencing the anxiety of a divorce is to withdraw from normal social contacts. One reason is that the divorce triggers a grieving process that I will discuss in the chapter on depression. Another is that the anxiety saps the child's energy to the point that there is little left to devote to friendships and social contacts. Still another reason may be that friends ask too many embarrassing questions that have no simple answers. Rather than face the embarrassment of explaining, the child prefers to be left alone.

The child may also become uncomfortable when traveling away from home or familiar areas or may refuse to sleep at a friend's house, go on errands, or attend camp or school. These reactions may be mild and can be treated with a little more pressure than usual for compliance. If the reaction is severe or persists, however, or if the resistance is very great and the child stops all normal activities, a professional counselor or psychotherapist should be consulted.

Dealing with Your Child's Anxiety Problems

While it is most unfortunate when Christian parents divorce, there is one major consolation in being a child of God: Our heavenly father does not abandon us in our failure. He draws nearer at times like these and, if we will let him, offers a strength, vitality, wisdom, and prudence that we don't experience as easily in life's good times. His promise is that we can expect "grace to help in time of need" (Hebrews 4:16).

Divorced Christian parents, however, often feel abandoned by God. They say things like, "Why would God help me now when I have failed to keep his law?" Or "I am sure God will punish me for not making my marriage work."

Nothing could be further from the truth! The *feeling* that God has abandoned you is always unreliable—a satanic lie. It may be a by-product of your depression or even the result of extreme exhaustion.

Before you can effectively help your child with his or her anxiety, or with any other problem, you need to restore your trust in God. How? Just believe that he wants to help you deliver your children into adulthood free of the cumbersome problems that are created by divorce. Let your faith do the walking and the talking! God will not turn you away in your moment of need.

In developing a strategy for dealing with anxiety, you should always remember that the root cause of the problem is insecurity, and I don't mean just physical or material insecurity. A child needs to feel emotionally secure above everything else. He or she needs to feel loved, not abandoned. A child requires a home environment that provides warmth and closeness, intimacy and openness, acceptance of humanness, and ready forgiveness for failure. These qualities in a home always produce emotionally healthy people. They should be the qualities that characterize your home.

Give love and reassurance freely. Spend more time than you usually do with your child and do not cut off your ex-spouse from contributing to this building of security. Your child needs to feel that both parents are continuing to stay in his or her life.

Turning now to more specific steps you can take to help relieve your child's anxiety, I would suggest the following:

Find out what is bothering your child.

Be an active and careful listener. Do not cut off the child, no matter how ridiculous his or her fears may seem. Be certain your child knows you are listening.

Evaluate your child's fears and be honest about which fears are legitimate.

You do not help your child if you deny that a certain fear has any basis in reality when, in fact, it does. Lying or covering up teaches your child not to trust you. Known threats are always easier to handle than fear of the unknown or problems that have been exaggerated by imagination. Anxiety is most often the product of imagined problems. When we know what we're facing, our internal resources are mobilized. We can then more easily take action, make decisions, or grin and bear the situation.

Give reassurance whenever it is needed.

You may need to give the reassurance over and over again for it to be effective. Irritably telling the child, "But I told you yesterday that we are not leaving this house. We'll go on living here," only provokes more insecurity by making the child feel belittled or put down. Patiently restate your assurance with words like, "Yes, as I told you yesterday, we will continue to stay in our home. You have nothing to be afraid of." This communicates a quiet confidence that reassures the child. Slowly, if such reassurances are patiently repeated, the child will come to trust them.

Provide a stable and unchanging environment.

Again, the cardinal rule is: *Change as little as possible.* Keep as much as possible the same.

To keep the environment stable you may need to set aside your hurt feelings and ask your ex-spouse to cooperate for the sake of your child or children. So much damage is done to children by the conflict between the spouses, so try keeping these feelings under control and out of the picture. If you can't control them, do not hesitate to seek divorce counseling!

Give more time and attention to your child.

This is not always easy, especially when you are preoccupied with your own feelings. But make every effort to set your needs aside for the sake of your child. I suggest this, not because I don't think your needs are important, but because the danger is that you will become too caught up in your own problems.

Avoid communicating your own fears and anxieties to your children.

While, as a general rule, you should endeavor to be as honest as you can with your child, it is important that you not communicate your own anxious feelings in a way that scares your child. If you are experiencing a severe anxiety reaction to your divorce, there is a danger that you will communicate these feelings to your child.

Some parents make the mistake of sharing how they feel in too much intimate detail. They need to talk to someone, and since their child is conveniently available, they dump their emotions on the child. This extra burden of anxiety usually only intensifies the child's insecurities. Every person in the state of emotional turmoil needs to talk to someone, but keep it to a minimum with your child. He or she is not your therapist!

Provide acceptable outlets for your child's emotions.

Older children usually find it easy to talk about their fears. Younger children cannot always verbalize them, so provide them with games, paper and crayons, puppets, or clay so they can express themselves in action or art. Do not criticize what they do. If they draw a picture of you as a devil, don't scold them; they are trying to express how they feel. Respond by saying, "Do you feel that I have been nasty to you? What is it I have done? What do you want me to do? Do you want to hurt me?" Asking questions like this can get children to express themselves in non-destructive ways.

But just because you release emotion today does not mean that you may not need to express it again tomorrow. Accept, therefore, that your child may need the same outlet many times over.

Respect your child's need for independence, even when he or she is searching for security.

If a child honestly wants to be left alone, leave him or her alone. Children differ greatly in their need to balance independence with security. They want you to be there, but not always in the room with them. Listen to what your child says and respect these needs. Do not withdraw your approval just because your child won't do it your way. A child's viewpoint is as valid for him or her as yours is for you. Accept these differences and go on loving your child unconditionally.

The Importance of Understanding

I have repeatedly stressed the importance of understanding what your child is feeling. Don't be afraid to expose yourself to these feelings. They are not "contagious" unless you are already experiencing them yourself.

Put "understanding my child" at the top of your list of priorities. Out of it comes the right attitude as well as the right behavior. If you really know what your child is feeling, you will always make better plans, and your actions and responses will be right.

When parents come to me angry or hurt because they are baffled by their child's reactions or difficult behavior, I generally discover that their confusion comes from failing to see the situation from their child's point of view. "He won't take out the trash but sits there brooding," one father complained about his sixteen-year-old son.

I talked to the son. His response? "It's the only way I can get my father to understand what I'm feeling. He won't listen when I talk. He only pays attention when I act like this."

Each and every one of us needs to be understood from our point of view. Counselors are trained to facilitate this; it is called empathy. If parents could use just a little bit of empathy with their children, they could revolutionize their homes! How do you do this? *Put yourself in your child's place.* Imaginatively change places with your children for just an hour—or even a few minutes. Make an effort to think what they are thinking, to feel what they are feeling, and experience what they are experiencing. It can mellow you instantly!

If divorced parents could dwell in imagination within their child's world and know intimately the concerns, fears, and feelings of their child, I doubt whether they would have any problem knowing what to do, because they would really understand what the problem is. Comprehending life from a child's point of view is the best training for a parent that anyone can devise. Understanding helps us to set aside judgment. It teaches us the language of love and makes clearer what it is we must do for our children.

When you think about it, this is exactly what God has done for us. He sent Jesus to live in the world with us so as to experience our pain and know it firsthand. Because of this he has earned the right to tell us what is wrong with our condition and to minister healing and comfort to us. Does anyone know us better than God or understand us more intimately than his spirit? Jesus himself said, "But even the very hairs of your head are all numbered. Fear not therefore: Ye are of more value than many sparrows" (Luke 12:7). I don't know about you, but I find these words very comforting.

Oh that we as parents could "number the concerns in the minds of our children." This is the deepest form of understanding. Such empathy and understanding would prevent a lot of the unintentional damage done by divorce. We might even be able to turn bad times into good times and help our children to be more wholesome adults. I know I would have benefited immensely from such a home.

CHAPTER 8

Anger and the Divorced Child

Every divorced child is likely to be an angry child. I say *every* because in my experience the circumstances surrounding the rare exceptions I have encountered are so unusual, they are not worthy of attention.

As I pointed out in an earlier chapter, very few children want their parents to divorce, no matter how much conflict is in the home. Older teenagers and adults may sometimes welcome their parents' divorce as an end to years of unhappiness, but in these instances the actual parenting stage has passed. In cases where one parent is totally destructive to his or her children because of a severe personality disorder, alcoholism, mental illness, or habitual lawbreaking, younger children might feel relief when a divorce happens. Even here children usually feel a lot of ambivalence about the breakup.

So whether the child wants the parents to stay together or not, a divorce is bound to cause him or her much frustration and hurt. There is a thwarting of life's purposes. And the invariable result is a state of anger.

Of course, this anger does not always show itself directly. My use of the term *anger* is therefore a broad one. I am using it in the clinical sense to denote the underlying, basic feeling of rage that can be totally masked, suppressed, or hidden and not reveal itself in temper tantrums and screaming matches. Anger can lie dormant and only show itself through negativity and moodiness. But just because it doesn't show itself in a dramatic or obvious way doesn't mean it isn't doing any damage.

These hidden and suppressed ways of expressing anger, often referred to as "passive-aggressive behaviors," can in the long run be more damaging than explosive, openly hostile behaviors. At least when anger is openly expressed, there is less chance that it will explode in unexpected ways or turn inward in self-destructive ways.

As I will show, however, allowing anger to be openly and frequently expressed is also not the healthiest way to resolve it. This pattern, often referred to as "ventilation," if repeated, can breed an angry personality—someone who is consistently mad at everything and who believes that the rest of the world has been conveniently provided as a punching bag for his or her feelings. Such people are a pain to be around, literally and figuratively.

Let me set down a biblical principle right at the outset: No one who is angry has a right to take this anger out on someone else. The New Testament is very clear in its teaching on this point. Paul tells us, "If it be possible, as much as lieth in you, live peaceably with all men. Dearly beloved, avenge not yourselves" (Romans 12:18–19). This was good advice in New Testament times, and it is good advice now. Parents have a responsibility to teach their children how to effectively cope with their anger and how not to let it become a destructive force in their lives.

When Is Anger a Serious Problem?

Steven is twelve years of age. He has never been in any trouble at home or at school. He has always been a loving child, obedient, and his pranks have been within normal limits. Occasionally he would tie a can to their cat's tail or place stink bombs in his teenage sister's bath salts, but what little boy wouldn't want to do this?

Shortly after his parents separated, however, his pranks took a more serious turn. The family car's tires were found deflated one morning. On another occasion, when no one else was at home, he left the bathtub tap running while he went for a long bicycle ride—deliberately. When his mother found the cat with its back legs tied together, she realized that her son was the culprit in all these pranks and decided something was seriously wrong with his behavior. Wisely, she sought professional help.

Mary is a child of seven. She is the youngest of five children and has always been a little aloof from the others. She resents getting hand-me-downs, but only complains mildly. "No one ever pays attention to me," was about as cantankerous a rebellion as she could muster. Nor was she very demanding of her parents. She tended to keep to herself, was self-sufficient, and compliantly did everything asked of her.

But then one day this all changed. Her mother had broken the bad news: "Daddy won't be coming home anymore; he's found himself a girlfriend and wants to live with her."

Mary couldn't, or wouldn't, understand it at first. Perhaps this was just a dream and Daddy would come back, she thought. But the days turned to weeks, and apart from an occasional quick visit, Daddy never did come home to live again. Soon he said he wanted a divorce. To Mary this meant he was also divorcing her.

It was then that Mary began to accuse her mother of "chasing Daddy away." She started to become disobedient. When told to go to bed, she would either hide or stay frozen in front of the television set. When told to pick up her clothes, she would throw more clothes on the floor. In fact, she did the exact opposite of everything asked of her. We call it "oppositional behavior."

Mary also started shouting abuses at her mother. "You make me sick. You make everybody sick. That's why Daddy's gone away."

The mother was at her wits' end. Should she spank Mary for this behavior? She tried that once, but Mary just passively received the spanking, behaving as if she enjoyed it. Discipline lost its effectiveness, so Mary's mother, out of desperation, just threw in the towel and left the girl to herself. What else could she do?

Mary's anger slowly subsided. With no one fighting her and perpetuating her hurt, she came to accept her father's departure as final and slowly began to reach out to her mother for love and reassurance. As a result, mother and daughter were drawn much closer together and found a new love for each other.

These two stories illustrate two extremes of severe anger reactions in the children of divorce. Both could have had disastrous consequences. In Mary's case a spontaneous and natural healing took place that did not need professional intervention. Steven, on the other hand, needed professional help, but the mother sought it in time to avert serious damage.

This leaves us with a dilemma: When is anger behavior serious enough to warrant professional attention? When can we expect a natural healing to take place?

There are no simple answers to such questions. Experts disagree on the specifics of when help should be sought. Some believe, and I tend to agree, that in *every* divorce the reactions of the children need to be carefully reviewed by a trained counselor or psychotherapist. Parents cannot always trust their own assessment of anger, because they usually have too strong a need to believe that everything is OK.

This doesn't mean that all children of divorce should be taken to see a counselor. But I am suggesting that at least one of the parents, if not both, should seek advice from a third party, preferably a trained and impartial person, who can help them decide whether or not a problem exists.

Are there some signs one can look for that could alert a parent to a serious problem? As a general rule I would say that if a child's anger, expressed as either total passivity or nonreactivity, or as behavioral acting out, lasts longer than four or five weeks, the problem is serious enough to warrant more expert attention than you can give.

Another helpful rule is to remember that about 23 percent of the children of divorce will have a severe enough anger reaction as to warrant some sort of intervention. Do not hesitate, therefore, to seek help if you are in doubt. Prevention is the best cure for the problems of unresolved anger.

Understanding Anger

To help you assess the seriousness of your child's problem, I need to begin by helping you understand the nature of anger better.

Anger is the most confusing of all human emotions, especially to us as Christians. The ability to get angry is designed into us by God and involves many body systems, including parts of the brain and hormonal system. Basically, anger serves a very important function, yet it has a tremendous potential for sin and damage.

Bringing these two aspects of anger together, its purposeful nature and its potential for sin, is a major task for every Christian who wants to understand anger. I don't have space here to elaborate in detail on this complex emotion. For our purposes, therefore, I simply want to point out that there are four causes of anger in all of us, and if we can keep these in mind we will be better equipped to handle our own anger as well as help our children with theirs. The four causes are:

Anger as instinctive protection

Built into all humans (and animals too) is an instinctive anger reaction whenever we are threatened or attacked. This reaction is intended for dangerous situations and is designed to give us the energy and courage to protect ourselves and our loved ones. Every policeman knows this type of anger. It keeps him or her alive in dangerous situations. But it can also open the door to a lot of trouble if it isn't kept in check. When this anger takes over, it can cause even the most gentle and kindhearted policeman to become violent and abusive. We blame the policeman, but it is really an instinctive reaction gone wrong.

Anger as a conditioned response

Anger is not only instinctive, it can also be conditioned or learned. Here is an automatic response to a situation in which we have experienced anger before.

For example, we may have learned at a very young age how to get angry at people or how to throw a temper tantrum. Anger has been conditioned in us as a way of manipulating people or for obtaining our way. Having learned to do this as children, we continue to manipulate people in adulthood. Sure, we no longer drop to the floor, scream, and kick our legs wildly. The adult version of a temper tantrum is the "silent treatment." We shut up and turn the cold shoulder so as to display our anger in the hopes that we will get our way, or if not get our way, at least to punish the offender. Married couples know this conditioned response well!

Anger as a response to frustration

It is a well-established psychological fact that whenever we are frustrated by a blocked goal, we get angry. This is a natural law built into us. Its function is to give us the courage to overcome the cause of the frustration. This reaction worked well in primitive times when it was a tiger and you stalking the same deer, and you were hungry and desperately needed to secure this catch for your family. Your frustration gave you anger and the energy and will to fight off the tiger. But the trouble with this type of anger, which is still with us, is that in many instances the obstacles are such that no amount of anger can remove them. They are people, not tigers!

By frustration, of course, I mean anything that prevents us from getting our way. For children of divorce, this is a major source of anger. Divorce sets up many obstacles for them and removes many privileges. It blocks many dreams and demolishes many ideals. What can a child do in the face of these obstacles? The natural reaction is anger, but often the child doesn't know how to express this anger in constructive ways. This dilemma creates more conflict, more frustration, and consequently, more anger. It is a vicious circle that seems not to have an end for many children.

Anger as a response to hurt

This brings me to the most important source of anger for all of us in our modern world, the anger that is aroused when we feel hurt. It is the most common form of anger.

The hurt that sets up this anger reaction can be *physical*, as when someone tramps on our toes. We immediately want to lash out in anger. Or the hurt can be *psychological*, as when someone criticizes or judges us unfairly. Of course, people don't hurt us physically so much anymore, they beat up on us with words! Most hurt anger is, therefore, psychological.

Why is this type of anger so damaging? Because the hurt we receive sets up a strong need to hurt the offender back, literally to take revenge.

So we lash out with equally venomous criticisms or, if we
back immediately or if it is not safe, our brains store the mem
hurt. We call this resentment. It is the storage of hurt memories with a
view to getting revenge at some future time.

For the child of divorce, any of these four can cause anger. Divorce
can trigger all of them even in the most placid of children. Fear and
insecurity triggers an instinctive need for self-protection, and a child
will naturally lash out at the very one on whom he depends for love and
security. Patterns of learned or conditioned anger can be triggered by
the loss of a stable home, friends, school, and financial privileges. Being
torn between two opposing parents can set up many conflicts and frustrations. Finally the feeling that you have been abandoned can cause
much hurt. Because parents are often caught up in their own hurts, they
can easily pass these on to their children without realizing it.

Anger As Protection

Whatever the cause, the anger is intended to be protective. Parents should
understand this. Your child, when angry, is only doing what he or she is
designed to do. Anger is essentially a warning signal. In this respect, anger is to the mind what physical pain is to the body. For the mind, anger
warns of the presence of conflict, hurt, or threat. God designed anger to
be a system of defense more than to be a system of attack!

Unfortunately, for most of us, the life-situations that trigger anger no
longer need this protection. For instance, our anger that was intended
for a more primitive lifestyle has to adapt to the more sophisticated,
psychologically oriented lifestyle of our modern times. Most of our natural means for expressing anger, such as lashing out or using physical
means for dealing with troublesome people, are inappropriate for modern life. But we still experience this anger.

It is important that the parents of an angry child understand this
dilemma. Every child should be allowed the freedom to *feel* angry. The
child should then be taught to express this anger in nonphysical ways.
The ONLY healthy way to express anger is *without hurting others*.

A child who is not allowed to feel any anger will only suppress the urge to act out in anger until a later time. Suppressed anger also creates a greater risk that the child will use passive and indirect ways of expressing anger. This may become a lifestyle. It is always healthier to be allowed to feel and talk about anger. When we can do this freely, the need to act it out in aggressive behavior diminishes.

Passive Anger

I want to examine passive anger in a little more detail here because it is so common in our culture. Unlike certain expressive European cultures (who shall remain anonymous) that prefer to explode and shout, we prefer to use passive ways to deal with anger.

What are some of the passive and indirect ways that children learn to express their anger? *Negativity* is the most common way. Have you ever seen a negative child? He sees the world through negative-tinted glasses. He resists all encouragement. Everything is seen with a pessimistic bias. The child seems to be constantly irritable. He withdraws and isolates himself, becomes critical of siblings and parents, and resists going to school or performing chores. Such a child is showing all the signs of suppressed anger being expressed passively.

Some angry children turn to more serious kinds of negative acting out. They become antisocial or engage in petty criminal activity—all as a way of indirectly expressing their anger.

One fifteen-year-old boy I worked with developed a compulsion to damage other people's automobiles. He would walk down the street in the early evening and deflate tires or scratch the paint with a nail. His internal, unrecognized rage was so great he just had to damage something.

What was causing this rage and why was he focusing it on automobiles? As you can guess, his parents had recently divorced after his father had left his mother for another woman. His father loved automobiles. They were the pride of his life. In a symbolic way the boy was trying to harm his father.

Even in such cases as this, the feelings of anger are natural and appropriate. What is wrong is how the boy expressed his anger. He should have been taught by his parents at a much earlier age to **recognize** his anger and **talk** about his anger, preferably with the person causing it. This is the best way to avoid passive-anger behaviors. This is precisely what therapy did for him. It helped him to openly admit his anger and find an outlet for it through talking. Shortly after he started therapy, his compulsive behaviors stopped.

How Much Expression of Anger Should Be Encouraged?

The sixty-four-thousand-dollar question facing every parent and counselor trying to deal with an angry child is: How much anger should a child be allowed to express in direct ways? Should a child be encouraged to vent angry impulses?

To answer this question it is important that I first distinguish between anger as feeling or emotion and anger as behavior or aggression. The feeling of anger should never be punished or inhibited. A child should always have the freedom to feel anger. In fact, the more open a child is in admitting when he or she feels angry, the better. Being in touch with the feeling of anger helps us to recognize that something is bothering us. It signals that we are being threatened or hurt. We should all learn to accept angry feelings, and then try to discover what is causing it. This then leads us to the steps we must take to deal with the cause of the anger.

But the feeling of anger also creates in us an impulse to fight back. We want to attack the cause or repay the hurt we've experienced. This aggressive behavior is what gets us into trouble. To feel our anger is healthy. To express it in hostility or violence is not healthy. This is why Paul says to us in Ephesians 4:26, "Be ye angry and sin not: let not the sun go down upon your wrath." The New English Bible translates this verse as: "If you are angry, do not let anger lead you into sin."

My understanding of what Paul is saying here is that it is not anger itself (as feeling) that is the problem, but the fact that anger has the potential (in behavior) to lead us into sin.

In dealing with an angry child, therefore, a parent needs to remember this distinction. It is important that you help your child recognize and talk about his or her feelings of anger. At the same time you must make it clear that certain kinds of angry behavior are not acceptable. A child should be able to say, "I feel angry and I hate you for what you have done," without the parent falling apart or becoming upset and defensive. This, of course, is not easy for divorced parents, who usually feel very guilty for what has been done to the child and whose guilt is usually intensified by an expression of the child's emotional pain. Parents must make a deliberate effort to set aside their own pain if they are going to allow their children a freer expression of anger.

The Father's Role in Dealing with Anger Problems

This brings me to a very important point that I want to drive home with all the emphasis I can: The father must play a significant role in dealing with children's anger.

Two of the important findings of recent research are that children are more likely to feel anger toward the divorcing father than toward the mother, and that anger problems are more likely to be present in boys than in girls. I suspect this is because we raise boys in our culture to express anger differently than girls and because it is more customary for fathers to leave home than mothers.

Whatever the reason, this research shows how very important it is for the father to participate in healing a child's anger. An absent father, or a father who has difficulty in dealing with emotion himself, is going to aggravate the problem further. So, Dads, keep your emotional life in good shape!

It is a lamentable feature of our culture that it teaches males to hide emotion. Men, as a rule, don't feel as comfortable with emotional matters as women do. This is why so many more women are willing to seek therapy than men. It's not because women are more neurotic, but because they tend to be more honest about themselves and their feelings and have the courage to confront themselves at a deeper level. I believe that men, because of their tendency to conceal their emotions, are generally less healthy emotionally. They are certainly more difficult to do therapy with, if you can get them to therapy!

Please forgive my generalization here. Of course there are women who have difficulty dealing with their emotions, just as there are men who feel comfortable with their feelings. Exceptions abound, thankfully. And girls as well as boys can display anger problems. But overall, men need to work at their emotional expressiveness more than women.

How can fathers help their sons overcome anger problems? Here are my suggestions:

- **Be available.** An absent father cannot help anyone. Spend time with your child. Once a week is not enough. Two or three times a week is better.

- **Be alone with your problem child.** If more than one child is involved, spend some time with each child separately, but especially with any child who seems angry. Just your frequent presence in the child's life, giving him personal attention, can work miracles.

- **Work at becoming a better listener.** Men tend to be advice-givers, not good listeners. Work at your listening skills. Ask questions that encourage your child to talk about his or her feelings of anger, and try to receive these feelings without defending yourself or shrugging it off.

- **Watch for indirect signs of anger.** Persistent teasing, tattling, sarcasm, negativity, and resistance are common. Sometimes the anger reveals itself through physical complaints such as stomachaches, asthma, vomiting, and sleeplessness. These are all signs of anger, so treat anger with all the patience and understanding you can muster. Try to reflect that you understand why your child is angry.

- **Accept the anger as normal.** Encourage the child to talk about it instead of acting it out. Never encourage your child to take his or her anger out physically by hitting you or any other person or object. Anger can be resolved by talking about it; it does not need behavioral expression through aggression. Vigorous exercise such as running or bicycling may help some children vent their frustrations harmlessly, but such exercise should never be a substitute for talking through those feelings.

- **Model, through your own behavior, how to deal with anger.** This is the most important thing you can do. Even if you blow it through bad listening or giving too much advice, if you can model self-control and openly express your feelings, you will have won the battle! Tell the child how you feel, but do not dump your feelings on him or her. Try to show the child how to be honest with his or her feelings without aggressively acting them out. Such modeling, especially from a father to a son, can be worth a million words.

Every child, not just those who are divorced, should be exposed to adults who can talk about their feelings openly and honestly. If a parent is incapable of this sort of sharing and communication, then take your child to friends or relatives who can and make sure that they spend time around healthy people.

This is the wonderful thing about emotional healthiness: It is contagious. It spreads through modeling. It affects every part of you when it is all around you. You can't help being healthy when you have to live with it every day. So, Mom, Dad, above everything else, work at your own healthiness. Your children will call you blessed for it.

CHAPTER 9

Improving Your Child's Self-Esteem

Divorce is never a pleasant experience, even when the spouses mutually agree on ending a marriage. When the breakup is full of resentment and bitterness, the consequences are potentially even more damaging.

A major injurious consequence of every divorce is the crushing blow it deals to the self-esteem of all those involved, especially the children whose self-concepts are still in the process of being formed. For them, divorce is a preamble to a chain of events that can leave permanent scars and deal irreparable damage to their self-esteem.

Damage to a child's self-esteem usually comes, not from the loss of united parents or not having a single home, but from the indignities caused by other people's reactions. The child fears what other people think about them. Adding insult to injury are the legal processes and the way the child feels battered emotionally. When children are treated like pieces of property to be bartered, when their feelings and wishes are ignored, when they are used as hostages by one parent trying to gain a material or emotional advantage over the other, or when a child is used as a weapon to satisfy an urge for revenge against the other spouse, you have a circumstance that has the potential to do a great deal of harm to the way a child values himself or herself.

Such behaviors should clearly not characterize Christian believers. They violate every principle of love taught to us in the New Testament.

And yet there are many Christian parents guilty of these abuses. To give them the benefit of the doubt, I can only assume they act out of ignorance. If they were better informed, their behaviors would have been different. Hopefully, this book will contribute to this change.

The Christian and Self-Esteem

There is a lot of confusion in the minds of many Christians about the appropriateness of the self-esteem concept. Before I can offer advice to parents about how to help their children to build their self-esteem during and following divorce, I need to first clarify a Christian understanding of what it is we try to do when we talk about building self-esteem.

Much of the current confusion arises because the psychological concept of the self and self-worth is not clearly understood. Biblical teaching on the basic sinfulness of the self and the human person is seen to be in contradiction to notions like self-esteem.

It is true that Scripture teaches us not to be self-seeking, even to deny ourselves. We are called to a life of self-sacrifice and consideration for others. But the word *self* means different things in each of these phrases. It is this difference in meaning between these different selves that is the cause of the confusion. The self that we deny is not the same as the self we affirm or esteem. The one has to do with selfish ambition and self-centeredness, the other with who we are as people. My book *Me, Myself, and I* (Servant Publications) clarifies this confusion, and I would refer the reader to that source for further information.

Suffice it for me to say that none of these biblical teachings is in opposition to the need every person has to feel valued and to have self-respect. The term self-esteem refers simply to the attitude we have toward ourselves—and everyone has such an attitude. In fact, claiming to have received God's forgiveness should have a dramatic effect on your attitude toward yourself. It should change it from one of self-hate and self-rejection to self-respect and self-acceptance. If God loves you, who are you to hate yourself? When you continue to feel no self-respect or self-esteem, you are denying God's love for you.

But the whole notion of self-esteem as it is presented in secular psychology does have some problems. This has led many critics of psychology to rightly question what is meant by self-esteem notions. Christian parents should be clear, therefore, about a Christian understanding of self-esteem.

It is true that there is a form of self-love that is not acceptable to us as Christians. It is a type of self-worship that places ourselves above others (even God) and causes us to selfishly pursue our own needs regardless of how doing so affects others. Some think that this is what self-esteem is all about. Is it? Absolutely not!

This form of self-worship or self-love is not the same as self-esteem. It is called narcissism and has long been seen as undesirable. It is nothing more than conceit rolled up in selfishness. In fact, it is really an exaggerated compensation for very deep feelings of low self-worth.

What then is a healthy self-esteem? It is how a person feels about himself. Each of us has a self-image, a picture in our mind's eye of who and what we are. This image is formed early in our lives, and our parents play a major role in establishing it, which is why divorcing parents must pay particular attention to what they say and do to their kids. As the child forms his self-image he also places a value on this image— either good, or bad, or somewhere in-between. It is this overall judgment of ourselves that forms our self-esteem.

When we say a person has a high self-esteem, we mean that he or she has a strong sense of self-respect and feeling of self-worth. By low self-esteem we mean that a person does not place much value on herself. Low self-esteem is really a form of self-hate. It is this respect for oneself, coupled with a high level of self-acceptance, that we should try to instill in our children.

A Christian Approach to Self-Esteem

My understanding of New Testament teachings is that self-esteem is similar to, but not identical with, the self-love of which Jesus speaks in Mark 12:31: "And . . . thou shalt love thy neighbor as thyself." The notion of self-love, however, causes me to squirm simply because I have no idea what it means to love myself.

In fact, when Jesus told his followers to love their neighbors as themselves, he was rebuking them. A more accurate interpretation of what he really said is: "You already love yourself so much, why don't you go and love your neighbor as yourself!" The primary emphasis is on loving your neighbor—not on loving yourself. Jesus assumes that we already do this!

Low self-esteem as we know it today was almost unknown in New Testament times. In Africa, where I have had contact with many people of different tribal backgrounds, low self-esteem is also rare. People derive their self-esteem from knowing that they are members of a great tribe that has accomplished many things in its history. Their self-esteem is derived from *who they are*, not from what they accomplish, which is the exact reverse of our culture.

In our society we cannot rely on tribal identity to give us self-esteem. We have to work to prove to ourselves and others that we are worthy, and herein lies many of our problems. The divorcing parent has to work even harder to protect his or her child's self-esteem because divorce will not only create feelings of unworthiness, but will also disrupt a child's ability to perform, with a consequent loss of good feelings.

Paul gives us some help with the problem of low self-esteem when he tells us, "Do not be conceited or think too highly of yourself; but think your way to a sober estimate based on the measure of faith that God has dealt to each of you" (Romans 12:3, NEB).

Here Paul is addressing the major self-esteem problem of his day—not low self-esteem, but its whitewash, namely, conceit. The remedy he offers is the same for all self-esteem problems. When he tells us, "Think your way through to a sober estimate," he is actually advising us to do two things:

1. Develop realistic self-knowledge (an accurate self-image), and

2. Have the courage to accept ourselves for what we are (total self-acceptance).

These two conditions are mandatory for developing a healthy self-esteem in all of us. So the task is to help our children develop an accurate picture of themselves, then to give them courage to be who they really are.

How Parents Influence a Child's Self-Esteem

Since self-esteem depends primarily on what sort of image we have constructed for ourselves, how and when that image is formed is crucial. Parents are the critical source of information to each child that tells them what sort of person he or she is. In divorce, parents need to double their efforts in feeding an accurate and positive self-image to their children. You are the mirrors into which your children look for information about who they are.

Children are constantly looking for evaluation and feedback from parents. "Daddy, look how strong I am!" "Mommy, see how I tied my shoes!" "Look at my school report; I did better in math this time!" When children are successful in building a healthy and accurate self-image that they can respect, it is because the parents have sent clear messages like, "You are a worthy person," or "I love you just because of who you are." Sadly, many parents send few positive messages.

Sam is the father of two boys aged nine and twelve. His own childhood was an unhappy one. His parents fought continuously and finally divorced when he was ten. He never forgave them for this and hardly ever visits them. He is angry most of the time and feels he is a failure in life. Although he is a foreman in a factory, deep down he believes he should have been something better, perhaps a lawyer or an engineer. He mopes about this often and quite unconsciously has developed a strong need to make sure his two boys make something of their lives. Without realizing it, he has resorted to using a dirty trick to motivate his children into becoming something. He criticizes them constantly, hoping they will rise and prove him wrong.

This trick has been tried since the dawn of time, but it has never worked. It didn't work when my father tried it on me, and it didn't work in Sam's case either. It's a mystery why it has existed so long.

Sam started when his oldest boy was four. "You're just stupid," he would say, thinking deep down that this would help his son prove to him that he wasn't stupid. "You'll never amount to anything. Everybody is better than you." Slowly he dug away at his son's self-esteem, feeding the boy distortions of who he really was and thus creating a distorted self-image.

Not all the messages were verbal. Scowling, pushing the child away, destroying projects his son had tried to build—all these actions sent messages as clearly as if they were being screamed to the boy: YOU ARE NO GOOD. But this mirror was distorted; he was projecting his own disappointments in himself onto his son.

When his second son was old enough, Sam started on him, too. Sam's wife didn't know what to do. She loved her husband but could not control his attitude or behavior toward the two boys. Understandably, Sam's two sons developed major self-esteem problems. It will take many years of therapy to correct their distorted self-images. Some scars will probably remain for the rest of their lives.

Most parents don't go to these lengths, but many, through their words and wordless messages, create in their children a distorted picture of themselves. You can never have a healthy self-esteem when you don't know who you really are.

It is important for divorcing parents to remember, therefore, that children can only see themselves through the reflections of your attitude toward them. They come to believe what you say about them.

Divorcing parents are particularly prone to distorting their children's self-images. This is because the parents are hurting, too; their self-esteem has also been lowered. Parents should put a guard on the messages they send that might damage their children's self-confidence or make them question their value as persons. Divorce raises enough problems for children without parents projecting their own resentment, bitterness, and anger on their offspring.

Divorced parents need to particularly be sensitive about verbalized judgments and avoid using labels like "monster, horrible, evil, devil, selfish, ugly, and no-good." Abolish these labels from your vocabulary when you talk to your children.

How Does Divorce Damage a Child's Self-Esteem?

Quite apart from the distortions to a child's self-image a hurting divorced parent may cause, there are a number of other factors in divorce that can undermine a child's self-esteem:

The stigma of divorce

It is quite erroneous to think that children don't experience divorce as a stigma just because divorce is common today. One father, in trying to justify his intention to separate from his wife, kept saying to me, "But Peter (his son) won't feel my leaving. All his friends' parents are also divorced."

"What difference does that make?" I asked. "It is probably a point of pride to your son that he still has a daddy at home. The fact that his friends' parents are divorced is not going to make your divorce easier for him to accept. It may even make it worse."

In Christian circles especially, the stigma of divorce is still very real. Even though I am a strong advocate of saving marriages, I wish we would not stigmatize divorced people like we do. Some divorces are inevitable. One cannot always control what a spouse does. Not every divorced person is to blame. But the reality is that one has to face some stigmatizing if you divorce. It hurts the parents, but it also causes the children to feel ashamed and less worthy as individuals. They may be teased by their peers or even shunned by some families.

Help for a child who is suffering from the stigma of divorce should focus on providing understanding and giving support. Communicating an awareness of how difficult it is for the child can provide some relief. It is important to remind him or her that self-worth does not depend on what parents do or don't do. Don't underestimate the power of your words of reassurance to correct a child's faulty thinking or beliefs.

In extreme cases where a child is being very badly treated, it may be necessary for you to consider moving to another neighborhood, church, or school. They don't deserve you, so find a place where you will be respected. Get your child out of a destructive and unsympathetic atmosphere while you can. A fresh start may help avoid long-term damage to your child's self-esteem.

Disruption of the family

When families break up, especially when some children go with the father and others with the mother, the stability of the family is disrupted. This creates feelings of insecurity for the children and undermines the foundation on which their self-esteem is based. When families are fractured, there is no longer the same core of reliable feedback that is essential to the formation of the child's self-image. When a home is conflicted or when one parent is absent, it takes extra effort and deliberate planning on the part of parents to ensure that children receive reliable feedback to form a positive self-image.

A climate of love is lacking

To develop a healthy self-esteem, a child also needs a climate in which there is honesty, caring, and a willingness to accept failure. In short, children need a climate of unconditional love. Even though a parent may not approve of everything a child does, there should be enough freedom to allow that child to explore new behaviors and even fail, if necessary. When failure occurs, love should be there to pick up the child and, in a nurturing, tender way, point him or her again in the right direction.

The model here that we must follow is clearly what God does for us. Without approving of our behavior, he is constantly waiting to pick us up, heal our wounds, forgive our failings, and help us start again. We call this God's unconditional love, and it is a pattern that every parent can follow when trying to build a child's self-esteem.

Before, during, and after a divorce are probably the most difficult times for parents to show unconditional love, although I know of parents in stable marriages who don't show love this way either! I once consulted with a couple who have had a stable marriage for twenty-five years but whose twenty-three-year-old daughter had gone completely off the rails. After a long absence the daughter had just returned home, remorseful for her behavior and pleading for a chance to start her life over again. What was the father's response? The father told me, "I just can't find it in my heart to forgive her. I am too angry about what she has done."

My heart wept for that daughter. How far this father's response is from the story of the prodigal son! How could a Christian father be this unforgiving? Was it possible that this very attitude was what had shaped the daughter's problems? I think it was.

The father defended himself. "If I forgive her I will be condoning her actions." He persisted in this rationalization even when I reminded him that God forgives us without condoning our behavior!

As we talked, it became clear to me that the real reason behind this family's problems lay in the father's unloving, unforgiving spirit. While he persisted in this attitude there was little hope of healing either the daughter's emotional wounds or the rupture in the family.

Many divorced parents develop such unforgiving attitudes. At first it is focused on the ex-spouse, but slowly it generalizes to include everyone around. To avoid this, a parent must be constantly on guard against forming an unloving, unforgiving spirit. Even if the parent's feelings of anger and hurt can't be changed, his or her behavior can, and the climate of love that will result will do wonders for the child's self-esteem.

The child's depression

Diminished self-esteem is one of the major by-products of every depression. The depressed person not only sees the outside world as bleak and sad, his or her inner world looks that way, too. And this is especially true for children who are depressed because of their parents' divorce.

A fourteen-year-old girl described her feelings to me this way. "When my parents told me they were divorcing, I didn't want to live anymore. I don't know why, but I thought it was the end of the world. Perhaps I was too scared to face my friends—I don't know. The fact is I didn't want to see anybody or do anything. What scared me even more was that I began to see myself as no good. I hated myself. I don't know why, because I hadn't done anything. I didn't blame myself for the divorce—I know I wasn't the cause of it. Yet I felt like nothing. I didn't want to get up in the morning or get dressed or even wash myself."

The loss of interest in life and in oneself is common in depression, and it lasts as long as the depression does. If the depression is not resolved fairly quickly, however, these feelings can become part of the child's permanent belief system.

Depression can start a series of events that can become a self-fulfilling prophecy. For instance, a child may be depressed over a divorce, fail to study adequately, and then receive low grades in school. The loss of face over these grades creates more depression and further feelings of low worth. The child's self-confidence is shaken, and he or she may become too afraid to study for fear of failing again. A self-defeating pattern of poor study and poor performance has begun that can become permanent if nothing is done to interrupt the cycle.

Depression in a child should be resolved quickly because it has the potential to create other, more serious, lifelong problems. I will be addressing these in the next chapter and showing how children who are depressed over their parents' divorce can be helped.

Building the Self-Esteem of the Divorced Child

Both parents should accept responsibility for building the self-esteem of their children. Even if the parent who has custody remarries, the absent spouse still has some responsibility for participating in this process.

My own stepfather was kind, considerate, and very loving toward me. In most respects he was the ideal stepfather. But he could never replace my real father. I needed my real father's approval more than his, and nothing could change this. A word of praise from my father was worth many hundreds from my stepfather, not because he was more of a person, but because I knew he was my real father. The absent divorced parent should, therefore, not underestimate his or her role in shaping self-esteem.

Before setting out the important steps for building self-esteem, let me summarize the major points of what I have said about self-esteem thus far:

- Self-esteem is how a person feels about himself or herself. It affects how he or she lives his or her life.

- Self-esteem is derived from a person's self-image, how one sees oneself. One's self-image is largely determined by what parents say or do; they are the "mirrors" that reflect back to the child what he or she is like.

- High self-esteem is based on a person's belief, gained from experience, that he or she is lovable and worthwhile. It requires self-knowledge and self-acceptance.

- Unconditional love, the kind of love that God gives us, creates the most stable self-esteem.

- Conceit is not the same as high self-esteem. Conceit is a cover-up for low self-esteem.

With these general guidelines as background, let us now look at some of the specific ways in which a child's self-esteem can be enhanced:

Be kind but honest in the feedback you give your child.

Since our tendency as parents is to criticize as a way of motivating a child, we may tend to be too critical. This is not honest feedback; it is often a negative distortion of what the child is really like.

Teach your child that to be imperfect is acceptable.

Nobody is perfect. The most beautiful people of all are those who know they are not perfect but who are comfortable with that fact. If parents can model this attitude, the child will have little problem with forming a healthy self-esteem.

Be careful not to communicate, even unintentionally, standards that your child cannot meet.

Unrealistic expectations can make a child consistently feel inadequate. My middle daughter had a very difficult time during her first college year as a psychology major. I was totally unaware that she felt she wasn't measuring up to my expectations, although she was receiving Bs and Cs in a very competitive college environment. One day she called me from college to confront me about her feelings of not measuring up. I told her honestly that I didn't care how high her grades were—only that she was happy in her schoolwork. My daughter's relief was quite dramatic. Once she realized I was not constantly evaluating her, her grades showed a marked improvement.

Build your child's ego with unconditional love.

Even when your own heart is aching, work at showing your child unconditional love. Do not withdraw your love as a means of punishment or discipline. Your child needs and wants your love regardless of whether or not you approve of his or her behavior. Give it unconditionally.

Learn to value what your child is good at.

If you value sports and your son tends to be an academic, you are bound to be communicating your disappointment in some way. Try to change your values so that they match your child's abilities. It is a mistake to force your child to be good at something for which he or she has no talent or interest.

One minister I knew wanted his son to follow in his footsteps. This desire became an obsession with him; he showed disapproval at everything his son did that wasn't consistent with becoming a minister.

But his son didn't want to be a minister. He was only interested in motor mechanics. He loved stripping engines, repairing them, and putting them back together again. Slowly a rift developed between the father and son that could have split the family. But the father was sensible enough to seek help and gradually learned to see the value of mechanical things. He asked his son to show him how he repaired engines and worked at developing an interest in what his son was good at.

After a while, the father found that he too enjoyed tinkering with engines and that he also was good at it. Auto mechanics became an interesting hobby for him. His son never became a minister, but he is a very active layperson in his church and now runs a successful motor-repair business.

In this instance, disaster was averted because a father changed his values to match his son's interests and talents. Christian parents must learn that they cannot force a child into a mold of their own making. The child must participate in shaping his own mold if he is going to develop self-esteem.

Help your child find compensations for the areas in which he or she is deficient.

I have three daughters. Two of them have natural singing ability—one readily admits she does not. When they were young, not having a talent for singing was a sore point for this daughter, so my wife and I set about exploring her other talents. We soon found that she had natural dancing ability and was a gifted artist. We shifted our values to include her talents also, and soon my middle daughter began to blossom in her own way. If we had not helped her find these compensations, I am sure my middle daughter would have become jealous of her two sisters and would have left home feeling that she was inferior to them. As it is, she has no such feelings.

Correct distorted peer feedback.

Children can be very cruel with each other. A child who is different— either in appearance or ability—can be treated most unkindly by other children. Be alert to this cruelty and correct the damage it does. You may have to say to a child, "Yes, it's true that you are not a brilliant scholar, but there are other things you can do that are more important." Or, "I know children tease you because you have a limp, but it's because they are afraid something can happen to them also, so try not to take it too seriously." Teasing is most times a defense against the fear that the teaser could also suffer the same fate. If a child knows this, he or she can more easily dismiss the teasing for what it really is. Sooner or later, the fear passes and the teasing stops.

Teach your child that spiritual values provide true inner beauty.

Whatever our imperfections, it is Christ who makes us whole. It is the person who feels totally self-adequate and perfect who has no need for God. Our children should, if we teach them correctly, come not to fear their imperfections, but to accept them as a part of who they are and learn to overcome them. Paul tells us that when he prayed for his imperfection to be removed (he called it a "thorn in the flesh"), God told him, "My grace is sufficient for thee: for my strength is made perfect in weakness" (2 Corinthians 12:9).

No self-esteem is complete without the wholeness that Christ brings. Without this wholeness we are always incomplete, totally imperfect. Complete self-acceptance is almost impossible without the sufficiency that comes from knowing God. This is as true for children as it is for adults!

CHAPTER 10

Depression and the Divorced Child

Peter is nine. His mother and teacher are concerned that he is not achieving at his grade level. A year before he was doing so well at school that he was placed in a class for gifted children. Everyone at his school believes that Peter is a child of superior ability. They are puzzled as to why his academic work has deteriorated over the last six or eight months. Even Peter can't figure it out. He knows he is smart, so why isn't he doing better?

Peter doesn't seem to be able to get up the energy to do anything. He hasn't done any homework for weeks. He just sits and stares at it. He used to be able to zip through it quickly and even enjoyed it. Now he feels like a zombie.

More recently Peter has begun to withdraw into himself. He refuses to participate in class events and won't talk to his friends. When one of them asks him, "What's the matter, Peter?" he angrily replies, "Stop bothering me. I don't want to talk to you!" Even getting him to go to school has become a major project. His mother has to force him out of bed and almost carry him to school. He resists every strategy to motivate him and frequently mumbles, "I just wish I were dead."

What is wrong with Peter? Does he have some strange disease? Is he showing the early signs of a severe brain disorder? His mother feared so and took him to see a specialist in children's problems. Examination and testing showed that he is indeed of superior intelligence but achieving far below the level of his ability. It also revealed that he was extremely sad. Lethargic is what the psychologist called it. Peter was also experiencing a lot of insecurity and lacked motivation. In short, he was suffering from a severe reactive depression—the label given to that form of depression that is a response to a major loss. It is the same depression we experience when someone we love dies.

What was causing Peter's depression? A few personal questions directed to his mother quickly revealed the cause. Six months previously, Peter's father began making threats about leaving home. Occasionally, at first, but gradually more frequently, Peter's parents began to fight. Not all the fights were confined to just hollering at each other. Occasionally they turned into physical encounters.

Every fight, however, ended with the father threatening, "I'm going to divorce you; just wait and see." To this his mother would reply, "Go ahead—see if I care." They paid no attention to the effect their conflict was having on their son.

Finally, Peter's father left home and filed for divorce. That's when the final straw broke for little Peter, and neither the father nor the mother realized that Peter's problems were related to the conflict and final death of their marriage.

Divorce As a Depression Trigger

Every unhappy marriage, not just those heading for divorce, places an emotional strain on the children of the marriage. The law at work here is a very simple one: The greater the conflict, the greater the emotional strain.

The strain is *not* caused solely by the separation and divorce. The divided house, the tensions leading up to the separation, and the events that follow all contribute their share.

Some parents desperately hold on to the erroneous belief that children are not affected by their parents' conflicts. I can understand this desperation. Their guilt is overwhelming. But it just isn't true, no matter how much guilt it takes away. Unhappy homes make unhappy children, and every divorce will take its toll unless some corrective steps are taken. The point of this book is to help divorcing parents minimize this toll.

What form does the emotional toll take? This depends on the personality and emotional healthiness of the children and on the way parents behave toward them. Some children develop anger problems or severe anxiety disorders. Others develop sleep disturbances or anger difficulties. Most will become physically sick at some point, while others will later become rebellious.

Whatever the specific outcome of the emotional disturbance, almost every child will experience a degree of depression. For a few—as in the case of young Peter—the depression will be severe enough to be the major focus of his disturbance. Peter will have difficulty with depression the rest of his life if something is not done to help him!

It is not my purpose here to deal with every aspect of depression. I have done this in another book. (See *Dark Clouds, Silver Linings,* Focus on the Family.) But I do believe that divorcing parents need to understand something about how depression develops in the children of divorce. Most importantly, parents, grandparents, and teachers need to be able to recognize depression in children and then know how to deal with it.

How Loss Causes Depression

The type of depression with which we are concerned here is generally called reactive depression. It is the depression we experience as a response to severe loss or even the threat of loss.

Most adults fear depression because they don't understand it. True, there are some forms of depression so severe (I wish we had another name for them so that we wouldn't get so confused about them) that they are very frightening. Paradoxically, however, it is these severe depressions that are the easiest to treat. They are usually biochemical in nature and respond well to antidepressants. The reactive depressions don't respond well, if at all, to medications, so they are harder on us.

At the outset, let me make this very important point: *We are designed to experience reactive depression.* It is not an accident, and we are not failures because we get sad. It is the way God has designed us to deal with life's losses. The Bible tells us that, "There is a time for everything, and a season for every activity under heaven." Especially, there is "a time to weep and a time to laugh, a time to mourn and a time to dance" (Ecclesiastes 3:1, 4 NIV). Reactive depression is all about grieving. It is the depression that helps us come to terms with our loss.

Reactive depression is part, therefore, of the grieving process. Grieving is more than just being sad about a loss, including death, but it is nonetheless a depression. It is the normal response we are all designed to experience when we have something we prize wrenched from us. Think about it for a moment. This is exactly what every child of divorce is experiencing—the loss of what he or she prizes above everything else: a united family and both parents who live at home.

Depression is nature's way of helping the body and mind adjust to loss. It helps us to find ways of getting on in life without the prized person or object that has now been taken away.

Why does divorce cause depression in a child? Because it creates a loss of many things that are considered prized or essential. The departure of one parent (usually the father) is a profound personal loss for the child. There are other significant losses as well, and we will look at these later in this chapter.

What Purpose Does Depression Serve?

This question has intrigued me for many years. I am convinced that depression, like many emotions, serves important functions if it is allowed to run its course naturally. What are these functions?

If we examine the major symptoms of depression we find that together they serve to protect us. They are not accidental but are designed by an intelligent creator to protect us in times of loss.

What are the major symptoms? First, there is profound lethargy—a loss of energy. Second, there is a loss of interest in normal activities. Third, there is a profound sadness. These symptoms all have the effect of slowing us down and making us lose interest in our environment. This forces us to retreat to a place where we can regroup, evaluate the loss, adjust to it, and then having let it go, return to normal functioning again. In a nutshell, depression helps the grieving process. Without it there can be no grieving.

We understand this well in bereavement. The death of someone we love is about as painful as it gets, and our grief is a call to adjust to the loss. For the child, indeed for one or another of the parents as well, divorce is the same as death. It is the death of an intact family and can create just as great a sense of loss and depression as real death. The symptoms of depression force the child to retreat from the world so as to deal with the loss. Depression is not an intruder here, but rather the process through which healing comes. This is why parents need to know how to help their child through the depression—not to bypass it.

In many ways divorce is worse than death. Death is final. You can't reverse it. You are forced to face the finality of the loss, and this forces depression and grief on you, which actually helps you to get over it more quickly. In divorce a child is confronted by a loss, but yet it is not a loss. One parent goes, but doesn't really go; in most cases the departed parent stays in the vicinity. The grief process begins, but it can't be finished. The loss is there, yet the child can still hope for reconciliation.

Because of this off-again, on-again state, the child of divorce is subjected to a series of contradictory losses and nonlosses. This is the worst type of grief a human being can experience, so it is no wonder that depression is so common in the children of divorce and that it so often leaves permanent scars.

The Other Losses in Divorce

It would be a mistake to think that the loss of a parent is the only significant loss experienced by a child. Divorce precipitates many losses. To complicate matters further, no two children experience these losses in exactly the same way. To help a child through a reactive depression, it is important to discover exactly what aspect of the divorce she or he is grieving over. It is not the same for every child.

What other losses are represented in a family breakup?

1   Sometimes there is the loss of other siblings, as when children are split between the parents.

2. There is the loss of the "ideal" home. An intact home with both parents present has an important symbolic significance for children. It is their ideal and preferred lifestyle.

3. There is a loss of hope for the future. Children are full of expectations about how the parents will fit into their future lives. They dream about it! Divorce shatters these expectations.

4. There is a loss of financial security. Most husbands start divorce proceedings by saying, "Don't worry, I'll take care of all of you. You'll have everything you need." It usually ends with, "Now you know this is going to be expensive and I'm not a millionaire, so you will all have to tighten your belts."

   For most children, divorce means a drop in the standard of living. A single, divorced parent is our newest poverty class! And this can cause a lot of insecurity for the children involved.

5. The saddest loss of all for the children is the loss of faith in their parents. Divorcing children often feel betrayed. It is as if they are saying, "You received me into the world and led me to believe I was wanted and that you would give me love and a secure life. I trusted you. I made myself vulnerable to you. Now you drop this bomb on me. You make me feel like I am an intrusion."

6. Loss of faith in parents can become a loss of faith in God. "I prayed for help that God would save our family, but God doesn't listen to me. I don't believe there is a God!"

There are many other losses as well, but space doesn't permit me to list them all. From the examples I have given, a parent should be able to identify other specific losses that a child is experiencing. For example, I remember that when my parents divorced I acutely felt the loss of my father's workshop and spending time with him repairing or building something. I was only twelve, but I loved making things with him. All his reassurances that the workshop would always be there didn't help me. The fact is that I didn't really feel that I belonged there any more. After the divorce, I would always be a visitor!

The Signs of Masked Depression

At the time of their parents' divorce, nearly all children are depressed to some degree. But children do not always show or experience depression in quite the same way as adults. They may be too young to have learned appropriate ways of expressing their grief. Because of their more limited life-experience and slightly different physiology, children often show depression as rebellion, negativity, resentment, and anger. These are referred to as masked, meaning simply that something else is masking a deeper, underlying depression. Parents often do not see the real problem, because they are focusing on the mask.

A recent case is a good example. Sandra (not her real name) was an attractive though slightly overweight sixteen-year-old who showed much promise as a musician. An only child, she was conscientious in her devotion to music; she had mastered the piano and planned on being a music teacher one day. She dated a little, but on the whole did not give boys a lot of attention. She knew her priorities.

But then the divorce struck! Without much warning her father announced his intention of leaving the home. To all outward appearances, Sandra took the news calmly and without much emotional upset. Shortly afterward, however, she stopped playing the piano. Boys became her obsession.

Six months passed before the real blow struck. Quite by accident, Sandra's mother discovered that her daughter had been pregnant and had had an abortion. Naturally, the mother was devastated. Talking to some of Sandra's friends, she discovered that Sandra had become sexually promiscuous. This apparently was her way of acting out her intense reaction to her parents' impending divorce.

In the months of psychotherapy that followed, Sandra began to reveal her deeper emotions, and the depression that was masked by her rebellious and promiscuous behavior finally emerged. Sandra's acting out ceased. She was now in touch with her true feelings; she could begin to work on them and move toward emotional healing.

Children mask their depression in many ways. They may regress to wetting the bed or turn in anger and attack siblings or friends. They may revert to being clingy and refuse to leave the presence of the parent. Other masks for depression are a marked deterioration of school performance and persistent requests for an explanation as to what is happening.

Occurring less frequently, but still serving as a mask for depression, are increased lying, telling exaggerated and often bizarre stories, obsessive or blatant masturbating, and food hoarding. The hoarding of food, often found rotting at the back of cupboards, is also a sign of a severe anxiety reaction.

The Signs of Depression

When depression is experienced more directly, it is much easier to recognize. Among the more important signs of depression are the following:

1. The child appears to be sad and unhappy, but does not necessarily complain of unhappiness.

2. Physically and psychologically the child is "slowed down."

3. The child loses interest in all normal activities and gives the impression of being bored or physically ill. This often leads the parent to believe there may be a concealed illness.

4. The child may begin to complain of headaches, abdominal discomfort, or insomnia. He or she may lose all appetite and refuse to eat or become preoccupied with food and overeat.

5. The child appears discontented and gives the impression that nothing can give him or her pleasure. He or she may blame others for this, complaining that "nobody cares" and projecting feelings of being rejected by parents, siblings, and friends.

6. Depression is both caused by and is the cause of much frustration. This frustration can make the child irritable, short-tempered, and very sensitive. The slightest provocation may trigger an exaggerated anger response.

7. The child engages in self-rejecting talk. He or she says things like, "I am no good at anything." Such remarks are indicative of self-rejection, self-hate, and self-punishment.

These signs of depression can appear in different combinations and may vary from time to time in the same child. A typical example of a clear-cut, directly expressed, depressive reaction occurred in Billy, a thirteen-year-old boy, whose mother was of Korean heritage and had married his father when he was in the armed services.

Shortly after the parents told Billy that they were going to separate, Billy went into a depression. In anticipation of what was going to happen, Billy lost all interest in his friends, hobbies, and recreational activities. He had become an avid surfer who spent many free hours at the beach, but that too stopped when the separation was announced.

To encourage Billy, his father offered to spend a day at the beach with him. Reluctantly he agreed, but when they settled down on the sand Billy refused to go into the water, saying that he was afraid something terrible would happen. His father became angry at Billy's refusal to surf, so Billy reluctantly picked up his board and ambled into the water to do a few token surfs.

At home Billy appeared sullen and sad. He never smiled or laughed. Since the separation announcement came just before summer vacation, his parents thought he would quickly get over his mood as he got into summer activities. They were soon to be disappointed! Billy established a pattern of getting up around ten in the morning, going downstairs to lie on the sofa and watch TV, then going back upstairs to bed late in the evening. He had no energy and no interest in doing anything. He spoke very little and appeared to be constantly sad.

The impending loss of home, father, and stable environment was too much for Billy to bear. His psychological and physiological systems did what they were designed to do: go into a grieving process. But no one realized that he was deeply depressed—and that he was entitled to such a reaction! He was blamed for being "a difficult kid" and his feelings shunted aside.

Helping Your Child through Depression

Every parent should be able to help a child deal with depression. It ought to be a skill taught in kindergarten so that children can grow up understanding that life is full of the potential for loss and that we should all know how to grieve.

While the more severe depressive reactions should be referred to a professional for treatment, there are many depressive reactions that can be adequately dealt with by a caring parent. Certainly, if your child does not respond to your attempts to help him or her within a few weeks, you should seek professional help. Doing so does not reflect poorly on you as a parent. You are not a failure because you get outside help. If anything, it takes a more caring and mature parent to recognize his or her limits and seek help!

Here are the essential steps in helping your child cope with depression:

Try to see the loss from the child's point of view.

Don't minimize it or make light of it. Try to understand what it is your child is feeling. This can be painful because it will only increase your own guilt feelings, but unless you start here you will only blow it.

It does not help, for example, if a mother says to her son: "I don't think that your father's leaving is such a big deal. He never treated you kindly anyway, so why are you upset?" Such an attitude, no matter how true the facts, only communicates to the child that you don't understand. For the child, the loss is very real and severe. If you try to play it down, your sincerity will be in doubt.

Parents differ in their ability to interpret the world from a child's perspective. Some are good at it, others simply are way off track. If you suspect that you consistently misinterpret your child's world, ask someone else to tell you what it is like and don't trust your own perception.

The problem can be further complicated by a tendency many children have to conceal what they really feel, even from themselves. I asked one mother who was getting a divorce how she thought her fifteen-year-old daughter was taking it.

"Fine," she replied. "She is more polite to me than ever before. So she must be doing OK. She can't be having any troubled feelings if she can be so kind to me."

When I saw the daughter, she spilled out her deep emotional unhappiness to me. She was in real pain. When I mentioned her mother's comment to me, the daughter replied, "Of course I treat her kindly. I want to protect her. I don't want her to know how I'm really feeling."

So much for that understanding mother! She was content to take at face value what her daughter was saying because that was what she wanted to hear. She totally missed her daughter's true feelings.

Accept the child's depression as a normal reaction.

By "accept," I don't mean ignore it. Just don't try to take it away or short-circuit it.

What usually happens is that the child's depression triggers guilt feelings in the parent who then, to relieve the guilt, tries to get the child to stop being depressed. "Come on, snap out of it, it's not the end of the world," is a very common response. But this only increases the depression because it makes the child feel even more reprehensible.

If grieving is a normal response to severe loss, and it is, then it is natural that your child must be allowed a period of grief to adjust to that loss. Grieving takes time and is best accomplished in the context of support and understanding.

Help your child experience the depression as fully as possible.

This is the step that really frightens parents. Whenever I give this advice, whether to parents or to relatives of depressed people, I get a shocked reaction. "But shouldn't we resist the depression? If we allow the child to be depressed, won't we just prolong the sadness?"

My response is to ask them what they would do if the child's father had died. "Sure, I would let the child be depressed because that would help the grief." Well, divorce is no less a death for the child!

As a culture we need to understand the importance of allowing the grieving process in all losses, not just those associated with death. Give the grieving person space. Allow the depression feelings. We need to feel our pain because this is part of the grieving process. So be patient and give your child space to work through his or her grief. The grief of a divorced child needs the same careful encouragement and help as any other grieving.

Avoid perpetuating the depression.

I have stressed that it is normal and natural for a child to experience a period of grief during and after a divorce. Theoretically, there is an appropriate depth and length of time that should be allowed for this depression, and children differ in their capacity to grieve.

How long should it take? There is no hard-and-fast rule. If a child is allowed to do his grieving fully and completely, he will complete the grieving in the shortest possible time.

The problem is that many parents are impatient. They usually don't allow the child adequate time to grieve. Or the child himself may resist the grieving. In many ways, therefore, the grieving process is interfered with and secondary losses are created. For example, the child feels rejected because he isn't doing what Mommy or Daddy is saying he should. This rejection is itself another loss, and it causes more depression. So the child's depression continues longer and more severely than it otherwise would.

Paul was ten years of age when his parents divorced. Both Paul and his mother became deeply depressed. Whenever Paul was around his mother and showed his depression, however, his mother would punish him. She did this partly because he was reflecting back to her how she herself was reacting, but also because she was preoccupied with her own misery and Paul's depression was too much for her to handle. Paul, therefore, could not grieve around his mother. He tried to put on a brave face, but since she was the only one who could give him the comfort he needed, he could not grieve in a healthy way.

So Paul withdrew from his mother, experienced this as another loss, and went into an even deeper and more prolonged depression.

Punishment and parental anger can easily prolong depression in a child. So can fear and insecurity.

Children also perpetuate their own depressions. Their imaginations, fed by fear, can exaggerate the losses of the divorce. If a child is not kept in touch with reality, the depression can easily be aggravated by all sorts of imagined losses. Parents need to provide reassurance, but it is essential that accurate information also be given. This helps to keep the child's imagination from running wild.

Help your child accept the reality of the loss.

Be honest and open. Vagueness and innuendo feed imagined fears. Without being cruel, gently help your child accept the reality of the divorce. This may appear to intensify the depression initially, but it will actually speed up the grieving process.

Often the problem is with one of the parents. If it has been hard for such a parent to accept the reality of the loss, that parent will naturally have difficulty helping a child accept it as well. So make sure you are dealing with reality as well.

With very young children the task of helping the child accept reality is not as easy as with older children. The child asks repeatedly, "Where is Daddy?" or "Where is Mommy?" These questions should be responded to honestly, but gently: "Daddy doesn't live here anymore, but he will be coming to see you soon and often." It's not easy to be forthright, but it is the best in the long run.

Build a new perspective on the loss for the child.

One of the major functions of depression is to give us time to develop a new perspective on our losses. Without it, we would be left with mountains of ungrieved losses.

I clearly remember that when my parents divorced, my saddest thought was realizing that our family would not be visiting my grandparents' country home for vacations any more. My brother and I would still go, but we wouldn't be together as a family. I had come to relish the three or four times a year when we would travel a hundred miles into the country and visit with my grandparents, often spending whole vacations with them. We would play games together as an extended family in the evenings, listen to the world on Grandpa's short-wave radio, and pick fresh tomatoes from the enormous, naturally fertilized garden. The figs from the large tree in back of the house were gigantic and sweeter than candy. Even the remembrance of them makes my mouth water!

But now that would all change, and I was confused about how it would now be. Since they were my paternal grandparents, would my mother let me visit them? Even if she would, I felt that the visits would never be the same again. Something had died!

Painfully and slowly I adjusted to this loss. My grandfather reassured me that we would still visit and stay with them for the school holidays, but we would do it without Mom, and this was painful.

What made the difference, finally, was the realization that what was most important to me was being with my grandparents, especially my grandfather, whom I adored. This freed me to see the loss in a new way, my perspective changed, and it brought healing.

An important way to help children develop a perspective on loss is to allow them to talk about it. This helps to clarify what they are thinking. When we grieve we need to talk about the loss, to relive the experiences and savor the thrill of time past. Speak to any grieving widow, and you will find that her favorite topic of conversation is past experiences with her departed husband

For a while then, the child may want to spend a lot of time talking about the absent parent or times of fun before the divorce. Difficult as this may be for parents, this is an important part of the grieving process and should not be discouraged.

One of the greatest blessings God gives us as his children is the ability to change our perspective on life's tragedies. Knowing God in Christ should make a difference in the way we view catastrophes. When parents have faith and Christian values, their children will be the beneficiaries. So, despite the horribleness of the tragedy, try to see your divorce from a new perspective. Believe that God will help you work out your future. In this way your child's depression will be greatly helped. It will reassure your child that you know that God remains on his throne and rules over his kingdom, and this rule embraces your tragedy as well. Your divorce does not dethrone God. If anything, it brings out his power and releases his healing in new ways.

Pray with your child.

Prayer brings healing. Prayer keeps us sane. Prayer helps us to see things God's way. So pray with your child. Don't pray *at* your child, which is so often how we pray with our children. Doing so is patronizing and not conducive to faith-building.

Depression and the Divorced Child

Imagine a parent praying, "Lord, help little Billy get over his sadness. If he were only a better boy he wouldn't be feeling this bad. So make him into a good boy so he doesn't cry." Well, I know such a Billy. His mother prayed this prayer with him often. He is now fifty-five years old and a top business executive, but he hates his mother for the way she treated him in her zeal to "get God into his life and his crying out."

What was the real message she sent to him? Subtly she implied that he was depressed because he was bad, not because he had lost a father. He also got the message that he was to blame for the breakup of their home—a terrible burden to place on a young boy's conscience. So pray with your depressed child, but pray wisely and sensitively. Pray that you will both have the strength to receive life's blows with grace. Pray for understanding and patience. Pray for God's peace to fill both your lives and for God to show you how to be loving and forgiving toward the one who has harmed you. Pray so that you communicate a deep and genuine understanding of your child's feelings. Every child will receive healing from such prayers and, at the same time, find a deeper sense of trust in God.

Useful Hints

In closing my discussion on depression and children of divorce, let me provide a summary list of useful hints that can prevent aggravating your child's depression.

1. Provide distraction for your child, especially during the recovery stage of a depression. As soon as it seems that your child is beginning to improve, take him or her on a trip, provide a new hobby, or increase privileges.

2. Work out rules that you can implement consistently and with gentle discipline. A parent should not allow herself to be manipulated by a child's pain. Understanding that a child needs clear boundaries and consistent rules, regardless of depression, can avoid catastrophic complications when a child has "gone too far."

3. Be careful what you say around your child. Put a guard on your mouth. Without realizing it you can easily make things much worse for the child. I once tried to help a mother who was in a panic because her husband was threatening to leave her. "Be careful how you behave; Daddy may leave us," was her constant message to her son. Statements like this place an unreasonable burden of guilt and responsibility on a child and should be avoided at all costs.

4. Respect the rights of the other parent. Accept that your child needs to love and must go on loving the other parent. To sabotage this will create a greater sense of loss and therefore more depression for your child. The child is emotionally the healthiest when there is a minimum of conflict between the divorcing parents.

CHAPTER 11

Your Ex-Spouse Is Still a Parent

Every child has a right to go on seeing and loving *both* parents. Divorce does not change this. This is crucial to the child's postdivorce development. It is the responsibility of every divorced parent—no matter how deeply you have been hurt, rejected, abused, or maligned and no matter how guilty the other parent is for the way you have been treated—to ensure that this right is protected.

Unfortunately, not every divorced parent wants to hear this. They would prefer that their child not continue to see or love the other parent. In fact, in an effort to hurt or get revenge, a parent will sometimes go to great lengths to set up obstacles between the other parent and the child. Abundant evidence for this is available in the stories published in every local newspaper!

Of course, this is destructive to the child. I would say it is also destructive to the resentful parent. Whenever you interfere with a child's basic right to love both parents, there is the potential for great emotional damage to everyone involved. In fact, as much harm is caused by the battles over custody and visitation rights as by any other aspect of the divorce.

Every psychologist or marriage counselor, after just a short time in practice, can tell horror stories about such damage. In some divorces, *all* the damage can be attributed to this factor.

Why do parents do it? It is not always intentional. I am sure that the average parent would not want to deliberately harm his or her child. No, let us give the average parent the benefit of the doubt and say that when they do something damaging, it is usually out of ignorance. Sometimes they have so much pain and so many problems in their own lives, they cannot think about what is best for their children.

Unfortunately, for some it is not just ignorance. It is in the nature of humans when they are hurt to feel the need to retaliate. In divorce, children are too often the unwilling weapons used by parents who try to hurt each other. Revenge is sweet for many!

Without the regenerating work of Christ in our lives, there is no way we can escape this natural urge for revenge. Sin sees to that. Even if we outlawed custody battles in the courts and forced both parents to continue to take care of their offspring, parents would still find ways of hurting one another through their children.

This is not to say that there are not legitimate times when custody must be an issue. Occasionally, and it is not as often as some would believe, one parent is not fit to be a parent. But parents must make every endeavor to take into consideration, above their own needs, the needs of their children. Too often custody battles are nothing more than personal revenge strategies!

What perturbs me most about these battles is that Christian parents often behave no differently from their secular counterparts. They too engage in bitter custodial battles, not out of consideration for their children, but for retaliation, thus interfering with their children's right to love and have free access to both parents. I can see how this happens to unbelievers, but believers have no excuse for harming their children in this way!

The Importance of Real Parents

There is, I believe, universal agreement among counselors that the most crucial factors contributing to a good readjustment by divorced children are a stable, loving environment and a continuing relationship *with both real parents*. It helps if there is minimal friction and if tension has been dissipated through a forgiving spirit.

A tall order? Of course it is! Difficult for most parents? You bet it is! But it is what is expected and definitely attainable for the Christian parent who has availed himself or herself of the forgiveness and healing resources accessible through Christ Jesus. In fact, I would say that this should be the goal for every Christian couple who, for whatever reason, plans on getting divorced. If you can't make your marriage work, then at least try to make your divorce work. See to it that you do the very best for your children.

Paul and Cindy, a Christian couple in their late thirties, were having a rough time in their marriage. Deep-seated personality differences and an inability to work out their conflicts finally led Cindy to ask for a divorce. Paul was devastated and deeply hurt. Basically an insecure person, he was frightened by the prospect of being rejected and of being alone. He feared he would never be able to build a successful marriage with anyone again.

Paul and Cindy's pastor worked with them to try and save their marriage, but without success. Finally, he referred them to a marriage counselor who also was not able to break the deadlock.

Cindy demanded that Paul move out, and he had no choice but to comply. Deeply hurt, he threatened to take the children with him, accusing Cindy of not being a fit mother. Their three children, a girl aged fifteen and two boys aged twelve and ten, became the rope in a tug-of-war struggle. Paul, now very angry, did everything he could to destroy Cindy's reputation. She retaliated with a ferocity that startled even herself.

The battle continued until Cindy eventually came to her senses and sought divorce counseling. Without condoning divorce, this form of counseling recognizes that when a breakup is inevitable, the couple must work to minimize the damage that follows.

The counselor helped Paul to realize he was hurting the children by fighting the divorce. Cindy changed her attitude to the point that she could cooperate in planning how Paul and she would continue joint-parenting their children. Neither had immediate plans for remarriage, so Paul took up residence a block away and set up a spare bedroom so that the children could stay with him half of the time.

With a minimum of hostility, Paul and Cindy carefully planned the details of visits, parenting responsibilities, and finances. Cindy agreed to work part time to help pay the increased cost of keeping two homes.

The effect on the children was dramatic. They even participated in some of the planning sessions and, by being honest about their feelings, helped their parents avoid misperceptions and incorrect assumptions. The signs of an anxiety disturbance in their younger son and of depression in their daughter vanished as if by magic, and for the first time in years, Paul and Cindy felt like they were normal people again. They even began to like each other.

What were the important principles that guided Paul and Cindy to an amicable readjustment of their family?

- ◆ Both accepted the importance of each child maintaining a continued relationship with both parents, even if one or both intended remarrying.

- ◆ Both realized that neither spouse stops his or her parenting responsibilities just because they are divorced.

- ◆ Both accepted the crucial role the father plays in the adjustment of *all* the children of divorce.

- ◆ Sacrificing personal hurt and needs for revenge, they both determined not to let their jealousy and competition for the children's love be a source of disruption in their parenting tasks.

- ◆ Realizing that much of what was needed to avoid damaging their children emotionally was beyond their human strength, they trusted God to help them overcome their hostility and fear. They had the faith to believe that they could do it—and they did.

When a Parent Remarries

Most real problems don't begin until one of the parents remarries. When both remarry a new game begins with new challenges and pitfalls.

The impact of remarriage depends largely on the age of the children and the degree to which the noncustodial parent continues to accept a parenting role. Generally speaking, the fact that one or both parents have remarried does not change the general rule that *both* real parents should continue to parent their children.

Take the case in which a noncustodial parent remarries. His or her parental responsibilities do not change. He or she may not be able to do all the disciplining, but he or she must share in the regular care, feeding, clothing, and educational responsibilities and must work to provide the emotional support base that children need for healthy development. A stepparent cannot provide all these needs, no matter how caring and concerned such a person is.

Regrettably, this does not always happen. I know of a number of Christian families in which the absent father, because he remarries and "acquires" children from his second marriage, adopts the attitude that his ex-wife must take all the parenting responsibilities for their children. "I pay the child support, you take total care of the children," he says to her. He then refuses to look after the children when the mother is away, and when the children are eighteen and he no longer has to make support payments, he abandons them to whatever resources they can find. There is little concern for the children beyond his financial obligations, and even this slowly becomes a vanishing point.

My heart aches for mothers who must bear the full emotional burden for their children and for the children who must learn how to reconcile their father's claim to being a Christian with his actions.

"I want my children to have a reasonable standard of living and do the things their friends are doing," one struggling divorced mother, who was near the point of total exhaustion, told me. She had been forced to go to work full time by a Christian ex-husband who had divorced her and was now living with his new wife in an upper-class neighborhood and earning an extremely good salary. His new wife didn't work; she stayed home to take care of the children from her previous marriage. My client, however, was struggling to make ends meet and was on the verge of total collapse.

What was her ex-husband's attitude when he was asked to provide some extra help for his children's educational needs so she could cut back on her working? "I have my own responsibilities. I can't be expected to keep two homes."

On the contrary! He is responsible. Not only has this man lost a marriage, he has also lost two beautiful children who will have great difficulty believing that the Christian gospel is anything more than a convenient myth.

What about the case where a mother (or a custodial father) remarries? Does the real father abandon his responsibilities to the stepfather?

In my opinion, he does not. Perhaps some parenting responsibilities are transferred, depending on the age of the child, but not many. Whether the absent parent likes it or not, each natural child still needs to feel that the absent parent *continues* to be involved in his or her life. This need is so strong that children who have been totally abandoned by a father or mother early in life often develop a serious obsessional disorder. They spend the rest of their lives looking for a surrogate parent, a substitute for what they have been deprived of. Their relationships often become overly possessive; they tend to be extremely jealous and have difficulty developing real intimacy for fear that they will be abandoned again.

Further Complications

The problem of helping a child develop a good relationship with his or her absent parent is further complicated when the absent parent moves away from the hometown. This reduces the contact time the mother or father can spend with the child, and the distance between them may set up barriers. It is a fact of life that people who don't spend time together grow apart; even parents and children will begin to feel like strangers to one another if they never spend time together.

Financial limitations may restrict how such a parent deals with the problem of distance, but with a little ingenuity a number of ways can be found to maintain contact. Regular telephone calls can be made. Have the children live with you over the summer. Extend business trips so you can visit them, or take your children on business or vacation trips with you. On my way home in a shuttle from the airport the other evening, the driver told how he regularly has one of his three sons ride in the van while he is working in the evenings. They love it, and he gets time to spend with them individually.

It is very important that the absent parent accept his or her role and parental responsibilities at all levels. Financial help, advice and counsel, and emotional support should be there at all times. If it isn't, a long-distance parent may find that love has been eroded.

The Loyalty Dilemma

Adjusting to life between two homes after divorce is difficult enough as it is and certainly confusing for a child. He or she is forced to make many changes. Most children don't get to choose who they live with, and there isn't always agreement between the parents about what is best for the child. Sometimes custody battles are used to settle these issues. It is a pity that the courts are used to settle these battles; it would be preferable for them to be resolved through counselors or psychotherapists, in an atmosphere in which the best interests of the child can be taken into consideration.

Whatever the outcome, each divorced child ends up with two homes and one big dilemma: "Where should I place my loyalty?"

In the early stages of divorce, children are likely to feel more loyal to the mother, who will be perceived as the more vulnerable parent. Later the allegiance may shift. Parents battle with each other to win their children's allegiance and to place blame on the other parent. If these struggles are not brought to a halt very early, irreparable harm may be done through forcing the child to take sides with one parent against the other.

Forcing children to take sides is an extension of the resentment and hurt problem. It can only be stopped by resolving the resentment. This may require professional help. But whatever it takes, parents owe it to their children to get their personal problems under control so that their children can be free to make the substantial adjustments needed to build happy lives for themselves. If parents would accept that every child must be allowed to love *both* the mother and father freely and without restriction or fear of punishment, the loyalty dilemma vanishes.

The Role of Grandparents

Grandparents are God's great healers. Even when they've messed up their own children's lives, they become healers to the next generation! Other concerned adults such as family friends and teachers can also be of tremendous help in bridging the divorce gap and in providing a stabilizing force in the tempestuous life of a divorced child.

I have already mentioned what a healing resource my grandparents fulfilled in my life after my parents divorced. They invited my brother and me to come and stay with them as often as we wanted. Their home in the country was always open for us. Whereas before the divorce we would only visit them over school holidays, once the divorce proceedings had begun they would invite us for weekends and long holidays quite regularly.

My grandparents' love and acceptance were comforting and reassuring to me. They never pushed me to talk about problems at home, yet they were always good listeners if I said something. They provided distractions from the emotional pain I was suffering, and above all, they restored my faith in God. I can't tell you how important that was! I came to see that God transcended the paltry problems of human existence. God was there despite what my parents were doing. His presence could not be destroyed by human suffering, and he offered dependable help in the midst of that suffering. I hope I will always be such a grandparent for my own grandchildren!

Some Rules for Improving Your Child's Relationship with Your Ex-Spouse

Stop bad-mouthing your ex-spouse.

Yes, I know it's hard, but you've got to get your mouth under control! Children don't want to hear bad things about either of their parents, and they especially do not want to take sides. Since they usually feel that both parents are to blame, regardless of the divorce circumstances, they are more neutral than you want them to be.

No purpose is served, therefore, in criticizing the other parent to your children. Don't be surprised if, when you attack your ex-spouse in front of your children, they will defend your ex-spouse and attack you back. Children have a keen sense of justice and will quickly punish you when you are unfair.

Do not use your children as spies.

A father might try to get a child to tell him everything the mother does—whom she goes out with, where she goes, what time she comes home, and what she buys. A mother may try to find out how much her ex-husband is earning, who his latest lady friend is, and where they go.

No child should be asked to act as a spy. They should be given the freedom to enjoy each parent without hindrance or fear of being cross-examined.

Children become very angry when placed in a spying position and can easily withdraw from both parents. If you are not sure whether you are using your children as spies or not, then ask them! You may be blind to what you are doing and so preoccupied with your bitterness and hurt that you cannot see what is happening. They'll tell you!

Encourage your children to call you on your behavior if they don't like what you are doing. You may have to be brave to receive their complaints, but doing so will improve your relationship with them immensely. Children respect honesty and feel better if you are open with them and nondefensive.

Do not use your children to carry messages to your ex-spouse.

There is usually a period of time following divorce when one parent is afraid to encounter the other, either for fear of letting out feelings of bitterness or for fear of what the ex-spouse will do or say. Under these conditions, a parent may become cowardly and hide behind the children. "Tell your father he hasn't sent the alimony check yet," or "Ask your mother if you can go fishing with me next week." These messages place your child in the role of having to act as a buffer between the two parents, often getting dumped on just because he carried a message. In Roman days, messengers who brought bad news lost their heads, just like children do today.

The child usually comes to resent both parents for having to carry messages. To avoid alienating your children, do your own dirty work! Be courageous and assertive. Speak directly to your former wife or husband and protect your children from being message carriers. This will free them to relate to both of you without hindrance.

Deliberately, and very explicitly, give your child permission to continue loving the other parent.

So often I hear a mother say, "But Peter knows I don't mind his loving his father. I'm not stopping him." This is not enough! Peter may or may not know that his mother doesn't mind, so his mother should not take it for granted that he knows he can love his father. It is more likely that she is sending a mixed message—saying one thing but implying the opposite. We are not always completely honest with ourselves, and we don't always know what messages we are sending our children. It is safer, therefore, to be explicit even if it feels redundant. Tell you child specifically that it is OK to love and go on loving his or her father or mother. You'll be the one your child respects.

Encourage your child to express his or her feelings openly and to tell you what he or she is thinking.

The open expression of feelings always creates a healthier environment. But freedom of speech does not mean freedom to insult or punish. Children are often so frustrated and angry at the world that they would readily dump their hostility on you and turn you into an emotional punching bag. This should not be tolerated. Anger should be talked about, not acted out.

But sometimes parents do not allow children to talk about their anger, and this eventually leads to a need to act out through explosive outbursts. It is far better to allow children to talk about their feelings *as they occur* than to have to pick up the pieces! Allowing angry feelings to accumulate, to the point that it takes a volcanic eruption to get rid of them, is never healthy.

Start to talk about feelings when your children are young and you will avoid many painful encounters with them later in life.

Try to be flexible in every aspect of your relationship with your children and your ex-spouse.

This can help you avoid many mistakes. Flexibility means that you are willing to compromise some of your demands and, if necessary, negotiate for others The most important area where you will need to be flexible is that of visiting rights. Conflicts with your ex-spouse in this area will always affect your children. They will create tension and interfere with the quality of the visits.

Perhaps this is the unconscious reason why many parents avoid being flexible—to keep their children from enjoying their visits with the other parent. This is not fair to the children! So be ruthlessly honest with yourself and work to avoid rigidity and inflexibility.

The need for flexibility should not be taken to mean that a parent should surrender all of his or her rights to the other. To do so would be to invite manipulation. But if you are going to stand and fight, choose your battles carefully. There are many issues that are not important in themselves, so don't stand on principle just for principle's sake. Remember, you can communicate Christian love far better through being reasonable than by being obstinate.

Encourage as many activities between your ex-mate and your children as possible.

The more time they spend together, the better. It is an unfortunate fact that most absent parents gradually become less involved with their children after a divorce. The initial frequent contact slowly fades away.

Fathers are more apt to maintain contact with sons than with daughters. Since both sons and daughters need to have contact with both parents, it takes a concerned and wise parent to be creative about maintaining contact between fathers and daughters. Personal bitterness has to be set aside and activities with both mother and father encouraged.

When Your Ex-Spouse Is Totally Unsuitable As a Parent

Everything I have said so far assumes that the noncustodial parent is *normal*. But what should happen if this parent is extremely maladjusted or immature?

At the outset let me sound a warning. Most parents are so bitter after a divorce, especially if they have been rejected, that they invariably accuse their ex-spouses of being universally disturbed or unchristian. This is usually the product of their hostility. They confuse their rejection with their partner's pathology!

This may not feel fair to some readers, but it needs to be said. No matter how badly you have been mistreated by your ex, no matter how abused you may feel or how disgusting your feelings are for him or her, this does not necessarily disqualify him or her to be a parent. How a spouse treats a spouse is not a reliable predictor of how children will be treated.

But in case my comments here are being misinterpreted let me hasten to add: There *are* parents who are totally unsuited to the parenting task. They could be alcoholics, criminals, severely maladjusted, brutal, or grossly immature people. It is clear from research data that children exposed to such an unsatisfactory parent do not adjust well. In such cases, the parent who has custody may be doing the right, and I believe the Christian, thing by taking steps to limit the parental involvement of such disturbed persons.

The custodial parent should not attempt to make this decision by himself or herself, however. Deciding whether a maladjusted parent is a threat to a child's well-being is not easy. So consult a therapist or counselor, or talk to your minister *before* you take any drastic steps. If your children are old enough to understand the issues, they should also be allowed to participate in the decision.

I have encountered many instances in which an ex-spouse is irresponsible and unsuitable as a marriage partner but is still a good parent. It is my belief that a parent must be *grossly* disturbed before he or she no longer contributes anything meaningful to a child.

I know of one case in which a father divorced his wife because she was mentally disturbed and had to be hospitalized for a chronic condition. There were two children in the family, a boy aged four and a girl aged two, when the divorce occurred. Because the mother was in a state psychiatric hospital, the father prevented all contact between the children and their mother. Many years later, when the children were teenagers, they demanded that they be allowed to see their mother. The reunion was very moving, but what impressed me most was that both children felt that they had been unnecessarily robbed of contact with their mother all those years and blamed the father for it. "No matter how sick she is," said the daughter, "I would rather grow up knowing who my mother is and what she is doing than live in complete silence about her. She is my real mother, and I need to know her!"

The words of this deprived daughter pretty well summarize my strong feelings on this matter!

CHAPTER 12

Becoming a Stepparent

Many divorced Christians struggle with the question of whether or not they should remarry. This struggle is not always due to a theological hesitation, but it often has to do with questions about what is best for themselves and their children. If you are struggling with the appropriateness of remarriage, I would suggest you consult your pastor or a Christian counselor. The ethical and theological issues involved are very complex and cannot be set down in a set of simple rules to be followed. Every divorce situation is different, and you need to determine what is right for you.

My focus here is on how to make the most of your parenting responsibilities if you choose to remarry. Your new spouse takes on an extremely difficult task as a stepparent. Perhaps you also take on stepparenting responsibilities if your new partner has children. You will be faced with a whole new set of challenges as you try to make your new marriage work. Stepparenting can be tricky and treacherous because the pathway is strewn with unexpected obstacles. With some extra effort, however, mistakes can be avoided. This chapter, then, is directed at both you and your new spouse. Perhaps it should be read together as a way of bringing about a mutual understanding of the task that lies ahead.

To Marry or Not to Marry

Before I launch into the topic of stepparenting, allow me to comment on the question of whether or not one should remarry when you have children.

It may seem to some to be a straightforward matter. After all, isn't one entitled to a happy and fulfilling life? For many divorced parents, the answer isn't clear, and they struggle to know what is best.

One should not lightly, or too quickly, jump into a new marriage. There are many issues to be considered, and I would strongly recommend that everyone contemplating remarriage should get some good counsel on the matter, if only from a trusted friend.

To illustrate the complexity of the matter, let me describe one case. Cynthia was a forty-five-year-old divorced Christian who consulted me on the matter of whether or not she should remarry. Together we prayerfully reviewed her life-history, her personal needs, her present family responsibilities (that included an aging mother who needed constant care), and her unique personality (that included a strong attachment to and a sense of responsibility for the care of her mother).

After carefully and prayerfully considering all the facts, Cynthia came to the conclusion that she should not remarry, at least not now. This decision could change in the future as her circumstances change. She was being sensible and rational about her life, not allowing her feelings and natural impulsiveness or insecurity to drive her into a second marriage. She felt the risk of failing again was too great!

I must say that I was deeply impressed with Cynthia's maturity. My natural inclination is to project my own needs into situations like this, and I always have to work hard to keep my own feelings out of the way. She knew best. Far too many divorced persons rush into remarriage prematurely, without weighing all the consequences carefully. Our culture puts tremendous pressure on us to be married, and it takes some strong resistance not to just do what others pressure you to do. Marriage the second time around does not get easier; it often gets harder! And if all the conditions are not right, your children pay the penalty for this second mistake!

Remarriage from a Child's Perspective

Milicent is an eight-year-old whose parents have been divorced for six months. Her mother has become friendly with a man, and about once every two weeks this friend comes to dinner.

About two days before each expected visit, Milicent becomes agitated. "Do you want to marry your friend?" she asks her mother, not once, but fifty times. "What do you do when you are with him?" "Why does he sit so close to you?" Bombarded with these questions Milicent's mother becomes overwrought and confused. She likes the man but seriously questions whether she should remarry. Her male friend has never been married. If she marries him, will he be a good father to her daughter? Will her daughter go on being so angry? Could it even be harmful to her? Questions like these flood her mind.

Over the months that followed, the daughter's fears intensified.

"Please don't get married again, Mommy. I don't want a stepdaddy," Milicent pleaded. When she started waking at night screaming from nightmares, her mother decided it was time to seek professional help.

Milicent's behavior is typical of many children of divorce. They fear having to deal with a new stepmother or stepfather. They fear losing their parent to the affections of someone else. They basically fear the unknown! So how a child's feelings are handled can significantly affect how your child adjusts to your remarriage.

Most children resent the intrusion of another person into their family unit. They naturally resist the idea of their parent falling in love with a new partner. While they generally accept that parents have a need to make new friends and widen social contacts, they don't easily allow it to happen.

What lies behind this resistance? There are basically four issues for the child:

1. Most divorced children develop a fantasy, if only unconsciously, that their parents will ultimately get back together again. Anything that obstructs this fantasy will be fought vigorously.

2. Children fear that a new spouse will usurp their place in the parent's life. There is an instinctive jealousy of *any* intruder.

3. Children fear that they will not be compatible with the new stepparent. After all, it is the parent, not the child, who selects the prospective partner.

4. Children usually see a potential stepparent as disrupting existing family patterns. They feel powerless to control or limit this disruption.

Of course, this is a two-way street. Often the potential new spouse is jealous of the children and sets up hostile relationships. The long history of relationship between the natural parent and the children may be resented by a suitor.

A potential spouse may also see the children as intruders in the dating relationship. Children demand time and take the parent away from dating opportunities. Children limit the privacy of dating. It is common, therefore, for the new friend to resent the very presence of children. This feeling is not always owned as such, and the children are branded as "spoiled, demanding, and manipulative!" Naturally, these feelings of resentment are reciprocated by the children.

So bad feelings between suitor and children are common in the early stages of building a new relationship. They spell confusion and insecurity for children who are already shattered. A wise parent will accept these bad feelings as normal and temporary but will seek to understand the apprehension and not get angry. By doing so you can avoid aggravating an already tense and potentially explosive situation.

Children of Various Ages React Differently

While there is no best age to gain a stepparent, the most difficult stage seems to be from puberty (around twelve or thirteen) to late adolescence (around seventeen or eighteen years of age). Very young children and those who are in college or who have already left home tend to adjust more easily, although initially they may protest quite vehemently. In-between are the children aged six to twelve who will have mixed reactions.

There are a number of reasons why adolescents find it more difficult than younger children to adjust to a parent's dating or remarriage.

Adolescence is the stage at which the child has the most ability to resist change. Younger children don't have the power to resist, and young adult children don't have to make many major changes so they take the changes in stride.

Furthermore, an adolescent is also more likely to have created a protective armor for him or herself—a facade of toughness, indifference, and denial. This defense conceals real feelings and slows down the whole process of adjustment.

Adolescence is also the age at which personality conflicts are greatest. It is tough for a parent to survive an adolescent's rebellion in the best of circumstances. Divorce and the addition of a new stepparent don't make it any easier to cope with.

Typically, therefore, teenagers withdraw and try emotionally to escape from the new marriage. They remain distant and refuse to be incorporated into the new family unit. The problem may be further complicated if the new spouse also brings children into the marriage. Children have to adjust to both a new stepparent as well as stepsiblings. Not an easy assignment!

With children aged six to twelve, the greatest problem is anxiety and fear. These children are not yet old enough to foresee the future realistically and may demand an excessive amount of the parent's time. They will either try to sabotage the dating or demand constant reassurance, or both.

These children may feign sickness at the most inconvenient times. They play hard to get, resist going to bed, and refuse to go to school. These are attention-getting tactics, and they need careful and skillful handling to avoid making matters worse. If the suggestions I will make later in this chapter don't help, then let me say again: Get professional help. It is easier to nip beginning problems in the bud than to pick up the pieces from a broken family.

Very young children, under five years old, are not fully aware of the changes taking place. By and large this ignorance protects them from much of the trauma of change. Provided the new stepparent accepts the child and a way can be worked out for the child to relate to his or her absent parent, the least difficulties should be encountered here.

Finally, don't expect ready acceptance of the new spouse by any pre-adult or adult children. The new partner will be a stranger to them, so it will take time for new relationships to develop.

Setting the Stage for the Stepparent

It is generally accepted that the way a previous marriage ended and the success with which children have adjusted to the divorce will determine the ultimate success of the new blended family. This is why some time should elapse between a divorce and remarriage. Children should first be given an opportunity to adjust to the divorce before having a step-parent thrust upon them.

Building a blended family is not easy. All your troubles are not over when you remarry. One study of over two thousand stepchildren, most of whom were the products of divorce, found that there was a greater amount of "stress, ambivalence, and low cohesiveness" in stepfamilies than in primary families. Interestingly, they also found that it was more difficult to be a stepmother than a stepfather, and that stepdaughters have greater difficulty adjusting than stepsons.

What this means is that if you are a stepmother to stepdaughters, you will have to work harder to build healthy relationships with your step-daughters than stepsons. It will demand a lot more grace, patience, kind-ness, and long-suffering and a greater dependence on God for you to make it work. I am sure you can be successful, but if progress seems to be slow and difficult, don't blame yourself. The cards are stacked against you. Don't expect a downhill coast but an uphill grind. I am sorry to seem so negative about it, but this is reality! Not all new spouses are that helpful once they have landed you. So be kind and forgiving of yourself. If the task seems hard, it is because IT IS HARD!

Most remarriages involve a mother with her children incorporating a new husband as a stepfather. Occasionally the father brings a child or two into the household, and very occasionally it is a stepmother who takes over her husband's brood, though this is more common after the death of a spouse.

The death of a spouse presents quite a different set of circumstances than divorce. Though the loss of a spouse through death is a terrible tragedy, remarriage is in some ways easier because there is no real parent hovering in the background and interfering with everything you try to do.

Perhaps the situation most fraught with pitfalls is the one in which a rejected spouse remarries before having overcome his or her feelings of resentment toward the previous spouse. With much unfinished business lurking in the background, this parent is going to have to fight two battles simultaneously: the ongoing conflict with the ex and the adjustment to a new spouse. Children are the ones caught in the middle of this conflict.

In one family I worked with, a fifteen-year-old daughter was caught in the middle of such a painful situation. Her mother, who had been rejected by the father, had remarried on the rebound and far too soon. Her energy was divided between trying to get back at the old husband while learning to tolerate a new one.

Even though she was a Christian, she could not bring herself to forgive the first husband for the deep hurt he had caused her. Finding a new and loving husband did not, in itself, resolve the deep hurt she felt over the rejection.

Knowing full well what she was doing, this woman used her daughter to hurt her ex-spouse. "Go and ask your father for extra money. He is the one who divorced me, so he has to pay for it!" Often she would say, "You don't know what a terrible man your father is; let me tell you what he did," and a long litany of infamous misdeeds would follow, most of it probably distorted by her resentment.

She made it difficult for the daughter to visit her father and often accused her of taking his side whenever she made a favorable comment about him.

But this wasn't all! To crown the daughter's misery, her new husband (who intensely disliked the daughter) would find little things about her to complain about. If it wasn't some hair left in the sink, then it was letting the kettle whistle too long after it had started to boil. He was a nitpicker par excellence!

Having to fight battles on two fronts took its toll emotionally on both the mother and daughter, and the daughter finally had to leave and live with her father. This helped the daughter, but it made the mother's life even more miserable.

My point here is simply this: The sooner all unresolved issues are dealt with and removed, the easier ALL adjustments to a new stepparent can be made by ALL the parties involved.

Matching Your New Spouse to Your Family

Not many divorced parents realize that they can INTENTIONALLY match a new spouse to their family. At least, one should try one's best to do so!

Just as premarital counseling is an absolute must for everyone intending to get married for the first time, I believe that remarriage counseling can make or break a second marriage. It is very easy, not only to marry the wrong person, but to get married for the wrong reason. Before remarrying, therefore, a divorced parent needs to face up to and do something about the unfinished business left over from a previous marriage.

Since every divorce is different, there are no universal laws here. There are, however, a few important points to keep in mind when thinking about a new partner. Watching your step can help you avoid a catastrophic mistake.

The drama of divorce and remarriage has three acts:

1. The children's family of origin is dissolved.
2. The children and the custodial parent reorganize their lives around a new center and find new ways of relating to the absent parent.
3. The parent remarries requiring the children to make a third major adjustment to their lives.

This drama requires time to play itself out. Prematurely forcing a child into a new family increases the risk of emotional damage.

Most experts believe, and this is corroborated by my own clinical experience, that it takes between two and three years for a child to play out the first two acts of the divorce drama. Of course, many parents can't wait this long to get remarried, but this is the time frame that must be taken into account.

What can a parent do to maximize the possibility of successfully incorporating a new partner?

Very early in the courting relationship you need to carefully assess how well your new partner fits your family.

Evaluate how suited you are to each other and how suited your kids are to him or her also. Radical? I suppose it is. But too much is at stake not to consider the suggestion.

Complete self-honesty is called for here, as this has far-reaching implications. If you allow the relationship to proceed too far before you consider this fit, you may find it more difficult, if not impossible, to extricate yourself from the relationship. A sensible decision *early* in your courting can save you a lot of heartache later.

Pay careful attention to how your children and friend get along in a variety of situations. Make sure you vary these times together. It takes a little while for friendship to develop, but if after many weeks or months of contact between them tension and unpleasant feelings still persist, you may want to consider terminating the relationship.

Intentionally prepare your children for remarriage.

Children need to know your intentions, so be open about your dating. Children also need to be free to express their feelings, fears, and expectations regarding how the new family will function. Allow them the freedom to express these feelings. Listening is the only way you can get at and resolve unreasonable fears.

Prepare your prospective spouse for remarriage.

Share how your children are feeling and how they perceive their future stepparent. Also, discuss the role you will each play in the newly constituted family.

Important questions to consider are: Should the new spouse change his or her expectations for your children? Should the stepparent take over certain parenting responsibilities such as disciplining, or should he or she remain impartial—a virtual outsider when it comes to discipline? Many serious conflicts can be avoided if these issues are talked about ahead of time.

Make sure you give adequate time to your children during the courting period after your remarriage.

Your new spouse should accept that you will need to share yourself. Your children continue to have certain rights and a claim to your attention over and above the rights of your new spouse. This is the price you pay for remarriage.

Do not surprise your children with remarriage plans.

There should be a period of open courting that can help your children adjust to the prospect of remarriage. On the other hand, don't introduce a new friend into the family until you feel there is a serious relationship in the works. Nothing can be as disturbing to children as to see parents courting a wide variety of suitors or changing "friends" frequently. If you are not seriously considering remarriage and your dates are casual, it is preferable that you not expose your children to these dates. Children should be protected from having to meet a wide variety of strangers.

Adjusting to a Stepparent

When you finally do remarry, your family will then need to make a series of important adjustments. These adjustments fall into three clearly identifiable phases.

First, there is the "honeymoon" phase. Everyone is polite to each other. The atmosphere may be a little strained, but no outward friction is evident yet.

Second, there is the "conflict" phase. The honeymoon is over and reality emerges. Everyone is short-tempered, impatient, and intolerant even of small mistakes. Little things irritate, and at times it seems as if the family will blow apart.

Third, there is the "contented" phase. If the marriage survives the second stage, a final contented stage emerges. All the necessary adjustments have been made, the corners have been knocked off tempers, and the irritating habits of the new spouse have become acceptable to all. At last, familiarity brings comfort.

Making it to the third stage requires careful attention to the following points:

Do not force a new spouse to become a substitute parent to your children, even if your ex-spouse has totally abandoned this role.

In my experience, this is the single most destructive issue facing a newly constituted family.

What usually happens is the following: The custodial parent is still very angry at the absent parent and labels him (or her) an incompetent father (or mother). Since the children will need a good male (or female) model, the new spouse is expected to "become the ideal father (mother) to my children."

Can a stepparent ever really substitute for the real parent? Hardly ever, in my opinion. There are exceptions, of course. The absent parent may abandon the children or may not be available to continue parenting. When very small children are adopted by the stepparent, he or she may be able to successfully take over the functions of a real parent. But in the majority of cases, the real parent continues to be around and should preferably take responsibility for discipline and parenting, jointly with the custodial parent.

Let me give a personal testimony here. My stepfather was a wonderful example. He did more for me than most fathers would, but right from the outset he made it clear to me that he could never replace my real father. I didn't fully understand what he meant by this, but it became evident over the ensuing years. The result was that, not only did I have a real father, but I had a very special stepfather as well. Instead of double jeopardy, I had a double blessing!

This does not mean that a stepparent should not help with or have any say in discipline matters. But any usurping of the real parent's role will only lead to trouble down the line.

Don't rush the second phase of the remarriage process.

Every stepparent needs to earn the right to be a friend to his or her step-children. You cannot force the pace of friendship. Pressure at this stage will only polarize the family and drive the first wedge into its splitting.

Keep communication with your children open at all times.

Know what your children are thinking and feeling and you will have no difficulty understanding them. They will also trust you more. Misunderstanding always has a lack of information at its root. Similarly, keep an open line of communication with your new spouse. Talk about what he or she is experiencing. This will help both of you keep the problems that arise in proper perspective, and it will help your spouse find ways to overcome these problems.

Don't take sides, either with your children or with your new spouse.

Don't allow yourself to be triangled between your children and your spouse. Try to remain impartial if it is appropriate. Privately, you may tell your children if they are doing something to hurt or offend their stepparent and do the same with the stepparent. If you keep your comments private and honest, even if they are words of chastisement, neither party will feel like you are siding with the other. Wisdom must be your watchword!

Remind your new spouse that it is very normal for children, especially in the early stages of remarriage, to feel a sense of betrayal and to be angry.

This anger will subside if the stepparent does not overreact with his or her own anger.

Keep all discipline free of anger.

Show your children by your own behavior that you can resolve your conflicts and overcome your frustrations without giving in to your anger. Your actions will speak louder than your words. There is just too much anger surrounding all aspects of divorce.

CHAPTER 13

Becoming an Effective Single Parent

Every single parent I have ever met has had one question on his or her mind: "Can I be as effective as a single parent as I would be if I were married." My answer is YES—loud and clear! But it does take some work.

Parenting is always a compelling challenge. It doesn't come easy for any of us. If you feel you are a perfect parent, you should offer yourself to the Smithsonian Institute for permanent display. Why? Because even if you are a pretty good parent, you never feel you've been perfect! Ordinary parents constantly feel like they are failing. It comes with the territory.

If this is true for married parents, how much more of a failure will the average single parent feel! Parenting seems to be more instinctive when there are two of you. A marriage partner provides checks and balances and different perspectives that help keep you on track. There is always someone around to tell you when you are making a mistake. But when you are a solo parent, everything depends on you—and only on you.

Single parenting is a far more arduous task than when you have a partner. But this does not mean that you are less effective in your parenting. It simply means you will have to be more intentional and more attentive to your parenting tasks. You have to be on your toes at all times and ahead of the game.

(171)

The Children of Solo Parents

Can single parents turn out great kids? You better believe it! Through the years I have met many outstanding people. What has intrigued me is how often it turns out that they had been raised by a single parent, usually a mother. I have made it a particular point of interest, therefore, to find out whether someone who is impressive to me was raised by a single parent. I am no longer as surprised as I was years ago by the results of my inquiry. With extreme regularity, I usually discover that such a person was in fact raised by a single parent.

It happened again just a week ago. I was speaking at a prestigious conference center back east. The person who collected me at the airport stood out immediately as someone I would label as outstanding. Not only was he a very gifted person, but he seemed to be extraordinarily wholesome and healthy. At the end of the conference, as he was returning me to the airport, I broached the topic of who had raised him. Sure enough, he had been raised by a single mother. His father had walked out of the marriage when he was only a baby, and he had not met his father face to face until he sought him out in his late twenties. This person gave credit to his mother for doing an outstanding job of raising him.

So, with a lot of conviction I can say that many of the most magnificent people I have ever met, including a few personal friends, were raised by single parents. Some had lost their mothers or fathers to untimely deaths, others through divorce. A few had fathers who had never married their mothers. They grew up with no idea of whom their father might be. The circumstances of the mother's or father's absence didn't matter. They still turned out to be incredibly gifted and competent people. A part of the reason for this may have been their determination to compensate for what was missing in their lives. I know that I did a lot of compensating. But I believe it is more than this. The parent who did the raising gave him or herself to the task with great determination to see that they did a good job.

Does this mean that one is better off in a single-parent home? Of course it doesn't. This is a ridiculous suggestion. For one thing, not everyone raised in a single-parent home turns out great. There are many failures. Far more than in intact homes, unfortunately. All things being equal it is far better to be raised in an intact home. Not every child in a single-parent home turns out to be well adjusted and successful. No, what I am saying is that being raised in a single-parent home is not a hopeless situation. A single parent who intentionally sets about being a good parent succeeds with remarkable regularity.

Creating a Single-Parent Family

For many divorced parents, remarriage is not an option, either because a suitable mate is not available or because they choose not to remarry. For these parents the challenge is how to raise a family as successfully as possible. It won't happen automatically, however, hence it is important to attend to the basic principles I will try to outline in this chapter.

There are two important points, made in previous chapters, that need to be reemphasized here, because they are foundational to everything else I will say. The *first* is that even though a parent, especially the father, may not be living in the home with his children, he is still needed to fulfill the role of a father in bringing up his children. *Second*, the way we have structured family life in our culture is such that most parenting responsibility falls on the mother. In some quarters, it is not politically correct to make such a statement publicly, but it is true, whether we like it or not.

It is unfortunate that so much of the burden falls on the mother. While it is changing, the working world and our cultural expectations for males still demand that the father be the primary breadwinner. This naturally takes him out of the home most of the time.

In our changing culture, the mother's earning potential is growing, and in some cases it is advantageous for the mother to be the primary income generator while the father takes on the parenting role.

For most situations, however, the well-being of the mother and the quality of the mother-child relationship is usually considered to be more influential on the child's development. This is true whether the mother is divorced or not, and whether the father is present or not.

Why am I emphasizing this point? Because the biggest mistake a divorced person can make, therefore, is to rush into a second (or third) marriage just because he or she fears being a single parent. *Single-parent families can function well.* It is not essential that a replacement spouse be found as quickly as possible to serve as a resident substitute parent.

Many second marriages fail precisely because one of the partners feels rushed into a second marriage just to ensure a two-parent home. Since it is primarily the absent *real* parent who must fulfill certain parental responsibilities for the child to thrive, marrying again just to provide a second parent doesn't solve the problem.

While it is true that a stepparent is not entirely redundant and can provide some extra help—mainly with financial resources, disciplining the children, and giving moral support and a shoulder to cry on—remarriage also brings a host of additional problems that can offset these advantages. So make sure you marry for the right reasons. Don't rush into remarriage just to get parenting help.

The Stresses of Single Parenting

In most circumstances the single-parent home consists of a divorced mother who has to work to provide enough income for herself as well as for the children. Not all divorced women work for purely financial reasons, however. Many work to maintain their sanity. Work gives them a sense of identity and fulfillment. Housekeeping can be a lonely task that is not always fulfilling, especially when you have been rejected and hurt through divorce.

But even if the job is satisfying and pays enough, it usually places demands on women that, according to a lot of recent research, are far more stressful than on men. This stress takes energy away from the mothering task. Personal friendships suffer because there is no time for them to develop. Often a woman's freedom, recreation, and free time are limited to the point that she becomes constantly irritable, short-tempered, and hostile to everyone—even her children. This is, quite obviously, not conducive to raising healthy children. Every single mother, therefore, needs to pay careful attention to how her work influences her parenting role to ensure that it doesn't become toxic to her family.

Becoming an Effective Single Parent

For the single father who has custody of his children there are similar stresses. He has to be sure that the children receive proper care while he is at work; he must do the household tasks after a long day's work; and he must provide the emotional support that mothers usually provide. This is not easy for anyone, and it usually means that older children must help by taking on additional responsibilities for themselves as well as for younger members of the family. Older sisters become substitute mothers and older brothers become substitute fathers.

Is this bad for the children? I pose this question because I have frequently heard the opinion expressed that children should not assume these roles. Well, I disagree. I think it is healthy for children to assume some caregiving roles. It is very common in many parts of the world for older children to help tend younger children. I grew up in South Africa where it was very common in rural areas. I always saw it as a healthy practice. The whole family, including older children, own responsibility for caring for one another.

Just two weeks ago I was traveling back east and had to stop over for a while in Chicago's O'Hare Airport. I decided to get a slice of pizza for lunch since there would be no meal on my next flight. While eating I noticed a young mother with two small children, obviously twins, and a son about eight years of age. She looked like a single mother (no wedding band and not well dressed), though I couldn't be sure. She really scratched deeply in her purse to find enough change to buy lunch. I wondered how she was going to manage feeding the twins. Both were hungry and screaming for food.

Then I saw something that brought tears to my eyes. The eight-year-old son, without coercion from his mother, offered to take one twin and feed her. With his young eyes full of love, he lifted the twin onto his knee and fed her bites of pizza. He let her drink unselfishly from his soda. The young child looked adoringly into her brother's eyes. After a while the twins traded places. Without that young boy's help, the mother would have been a nervous wreck. As it turned out, all was calm.

They finished eating before me and as they walked away, the young boy carrying his sister on his hip, I felt a great sense of pride in that family. There was no father, and they certainly did not have a lot of this world's material blessings, but they had that indefinable something that helps to produce outstanding people. As I walked away I prayed that God would keep them that way the rest of their lives. You'll never convince me that siblings helping each other is bad for a family!

Some of the problems brought on by the single-parenting task can be lessened by arranging for the custodial parent (usually the mother) to work part time, if at all possible, and by planning evenings and weekends in such a way that parents and children are able to spend quality time together. While no single parent should allow children to manipulate him or her into giving them *all* his or her spare time, deliberate planning of outings and recreational activities can help to structure some sorely needed "alone" time. Remember: You don't owe your kids all your free time. Kids must learn to entertain themselves, not always be entertained by parents. Also, the absent parent should realize that he or she has a responsibility to assist here and provide relief by being available to take up some slack when the many duties of single parenting become too exhausting.

The Question of Remarriage

There is one category of single parenting that is particularly stressful and deserves special mention here. Research being conducted at the University of Pennsylvania School of Medicine in Philadelphia indicates that those children whose mothers had not remarried, but were living with their new partners, were more maladjusted than the children in any other blended arrangement. (Maria Isaacs and George Leon, *Journal of Marital and Family Therapy* April 1988, vol. 14(2), 163–73.)

As a general rule, this means that it is better for the adjustment of the children for a divorced parent who is living with a partner to remarry than to just live with the partner. It is not hard to understand why the research shows this to be beneficial. Apart from the morality of it all, living with a partner creates an atmosphere of temporariness that is not conducive to stability. Children feel more insecure, unstable. They feel like they are just camping out, waiting to move on to a new home situation. Marriage creates an atmosphere of stability that helps children through their difficult times.

Living together, unmarried, also confuses many roles. Is the partner a stepfather? Is she a stepmother? Children become confused about their rights in an unmarried home. Whose home are they living in? What rights do they have? If it is their original home, then where does the "boarder" fit in? Children resent an intruder who claims to be a part of a home where there is no basis in marriage for his presence.

Now don't take my advice here as a mandate to marry under any circumstance. I am only saying that for the sake of your children, either get married because you really want to or live apart from anyone you are dating until such time as you are clear about your marital future. Nothing less is good enough for raising your children.

To Work or Not to Work

Not every single mom has a choice as to whether to work or not. Usually divorce lowers the standard of living for all the parties involved, so working is mandatory, not an option. However, work and family life interact quite dramatically for the single mother, more so than for the married mother.

Does being a working single mother enhance your health or threaten it? In professional circles the issue is now being hotly debated. At issue are two competing hypotheses. The first says that all people only have a limited amount of time and energy and that having too many competing demands and conflicting roles causes stress and overloads those systems that help us in stress. In other words, we are not built for unlimited demands. Since being a single mother is demanding and full of role conflicts, single mothers must be careful about how much they try to do.

The second hypothesis says that greater self-esteem and social support are to be gained from greater demands and multiple roles, and these outweigh the costs of the extra burdens.

Which hypothesis is true? Like so many aspects of life, both are true. There is no doubt that having children gives working women a mental and emotional boost that childless women lack. But having children also increases work and strain within the family, and this indirectly increases stress and overload.

The boost to self-esteem, therefore, that comes from having many demands on you and feeling needed has its limits. It works fine as long as you are able to stay within the limits of your energy and coping skills. Beyond this point too many demands are destructive. The limits are set by your unique energy level and abilities. No one else is the same as you!

What is so often overlooked in such theorizing is the interactive effect with other life factors. If you are financially secure and don't really need to work, work is less stressful and meets your deeper needs for fulfillment and identity. You can come home at the end of a workday and have lots of energy for your kids.

Now what we have learned is this: The interactive effect between home and work is far more damaging to women than to men. Women, generally, have a harder time unwinding from a stressful day at work than men. They tend, according to the researchers, to take their work more seriously. Men tend to be more selective about problems in the work situation.

All this is to say that women have to work harder at setting emotional boundaries between their work and their homelife than men. Here are some suggestions that can help you do this.

Each day as you return home from work, do a mental wash.

Use the travel time on the bus, train, freeway, or walking to review all the issues that seem to have clung to you. Take them off your mind. If you need to remember something for the next day, write it down in a notebook. A mental wash is similar to the decontamination process that some workers go through who work in toxic environments. They strip and cleanse everything. They take no poison home. Only your decontamination needs to be mental. Leave your job at work. Don't take your problems home with you. Since you are your child's only resident parent, your child needs your 100 percent attention. Give it to them as best you can.

Severely restrict the amount of overtime you work.

It has been found that working mothers who put in overtime at their jobs have more stress, including over the weekends, than fathers, even though the fathers have worked more overtime. For single mothers, weekends are important for catching up on chores and social events. Furthermore, stress for women tends to be more cumulative than for men. Home and work stress combine to produce greater stress in women. This may just be a consequence of the changing status of women in the workplace, but for now it is a reality that every single mother must live with.

Downsize your expectations for being Supermom.

The best mothers are those who do what they have to do without a lot of self-reflection. Your mothering role should be transparent. If you try too hard, you are more likely to make mistakes than if you relax and do what comes naturally.

It would be nice if you could win all the trophies for being the best at everything and have the world applaud your significant and prolific accomplishments. But you may only be setting yourself up for emotional trouble. Your personal well-being is worth far more than all the applause the world can give you, so keep your expectations down to reasonable and achievable limits.

If possible, consider working out of your home or being self-employed.

Today, more and more jobs allow for flexible working hours and locations. People who are self-employed or who work out of their homes experience more job satisfaction and less job stress. The impact on improving family relationships can be quite dramatic.

Of course, there are some potential problems here. If children are still at home and demand a lot of your time, stress can intensify. If you are a very social person, working alone at home can drive you crazy. But if your job stress is really out of control or your work situation is extremely unpleasant, there may be some advantages in considering some new working arrangements that will leave you at home more or give you greater flexibility.

Build a good, reliable support system for yourself.

What single parents lack more than anything else is close, reliable friendships. Seek out such friendships and cultivate them by assigning them the highest priority. I know it will take time, time that otherwise could be given to your children, but it will be time well spent. Close friendships help us restore perspective, drain away our conflicts, and restore faith in ourselves and God.

Single Fathers

It would be remiss of me to leave the impression that only mothers have to raise children as single parents. After years of neglect by lawmakers, researchers, and therapists, interest in fathering has come to the forefront. The number of fathers raising children alone following divorce has more than tripled between 1970 and 1990 and is continuing to grow. The overall conclusion of those who have studied solo fathering is that it can be successful, despite the role ambiguities associated with it. In particular, though, fathers have difficulties balancing work and childcare, finding time to be with their children, and reestablishing social contacts. Fathers who choose their role of parenting seem to make a better job of it than fathers who are forced by the abandonment of the mother to take on this role.

There are those who would question whether a father can provide the right type of nurturing, expressive love that a mother can. Clearly some fathers can't, so they need to get help from other family members to ensure that their children get exposure to a variety of love styles.

Increasingly, though, men are discovering the deeper dimensions to their love and that it can be nurturing and spiritually powerful. I would strongly recommend to fathers who have primary parental responsibilities that they seek out a support group for single fathers (many churches now have these) so that they can learn to open up the expressive love side of their natures. It doesn't come naturally to men; we need tutoring. And good fathering is not only knowing how to listen to your kids and how to join in their fun, important as this may be, but also in knowing how to show and express love openly. It can certainly feel awkward when you first attempt to be more expressive in your nurturing.

Since men are more likely to use the Internet as a resource than say the local library or bookstore, I can recommend several resources available on the Net to both my male and female readers. You can use a search program like Yahoo to find any topic you want. Consult a local computer software store for information about such search programs; there are several available at a very low cost. I did a quick search and found a lot of useful information for single parents on *http://www.xensei.com/ users/ileneh/parent.html*. You will find information on single fathering, support groups, and resources, the likes of which were not so readily available a year or two ago and are certainly not available in your local library or bookstore. There are single parent associations, networks, resource centers, and round tables galore, all with excellent materials available right on the Internet. There is no point in reinventing the wheel as a single father. You can benefit from the experience of others.

You Are Still a Family

One of the most important emphases to emerge recently in the area of single parenting is to make sure that you see your children and yourself *as a family*. Too often, single parents fail to identify themselves as a family.

Jim Smoke, one of our leading Christian authorities on adult singleness, in an article published in Focus on the Family's premier issue of *Single-Parent Family* (October 1994,) makes this point quite effectively. For many single parents, he writes, "The dream of a warm and wonderful all-American family slipped over the horizon when the sun set in divorce. In its place has come the stark reality of too little money and too many needs. In the crush of daily pressures there seems to be not enough quality time for family fun and emotional closeness. Many come to believe that they are not a family anymore, just a few hangers on to the skeleton of what could have been!"

Jim rightly calls single parents to once again claim the right to be called a family and to begin to feel like one.

How can a single parent do this? By building a stronger family awareness. By calling yourselves a family, with sincerity and persistence you can make sure that your children come to believe it. Use the word *family* often. Embrace your larger family of origin, your extended family, as part of your nuclear family. Don't refer to yourselves as a broken family. Your marriage may have failed, but the kids and you still constitute a family.

Here are some practical suggestions offered by Jim Smoke for how to function as a family, with a few of my own added for good measure:

Plan family outings where every member participates in some way.

Don't go fishing if one member doesn't like doing it. Find something ALL can enjoy. Use a democratic process for voting on what involves the most family members.

Visit your extended family often.

I recall how beneficial this was to me. We visited aunts and uncles, grand-parents, and even distant relatives often. This gave me a sense of the larger family to which I belonged.

Support one another at school, sporting, or other events.

Be there for one another. Become each other's cheerleaders. Encourage each other in everything you do.

Keep up all your cherished family traditions.

Often, single-parent families drop out of family traditions. Make every effort to keep them going. Don't hesitate to start some new ones as well.

Keep your family's spiritual growth progressing together.

Keep up your devotional times, prayer times, church times. Do church things together with other families to demonstrate that you are also a family. Ignore any paranoid or self-conscious feelings your mind may come up with!

Create a happy and humorous home atmosphere.

Single-parent homes can easily become places of gloom. Laughter is a scarce commodity these days anyway, but nowhere can it be scarcer than in divorced homes. So liven things up a bit. Play pranks on one another. Invent funny jokes, play games full of laughter. Watch Laurel and Hardy movies. Giggle more, cry less. Laughter is a good medicine for body and spirit.

The Church Could Help More

Throughout this book I have tried to show how parents and other caring adults can help children through the trauma of divorce and how to minimize the emotional damage that might ensue. I am convinced that the Christian church can, and should, play an important role in this important task. Many churches ignore the special needs of divorced families. If yours is such a church, talk to your pastor and see if some change can be fostered. If not, find one that does. The well-being of your family must come before loyalty to any local body of people calling themselves a church.

For any pastors or church leaders who might be reading this book, as well as concerned single parents who want some ideas on how to change things, here are some specific ways churches can be of assistance.

Churches must be tutored to accept the children of divorce and their parents with a lot more love and forgiveness.

I have heard some real horror stories when it comes to how churches treat single parents, especially divorced single parents. Such churches need to be ashamed of their unloving and unbecoming behavior. No matter how Christians feel about divorce itself, it is clear that there are always innocent casualties and children are its innocent victims. I believe that the church, by accepting without stigma, the children of divorce and by extending God's forgiveness to the parents, can play an important role in facilitating their healing and growth. Who knows, the church might grow a little healthier itself through this outreach. Such love and acceptance can also serve to win the children of divorce to faith as well. Many of them lose confidence in a loving God.

Pastors can be more understanding of the pressures experienced by divorced single parents and can organize support groups for them.

The current practice of clumping single parents, divorced people without children, and those who have never married into the same singles group is not always the best way to provide help. The circumstances of these three groups are too different to be treated as the same. Each should have their own support system. Single parents need to be cared for separately from other single groups. They need childcare help, baby-sitters, to be with regular families more, and a lot of support and encouragement.

Pastors can also work at shaping the attitude of absent parents (especially fathers) toward owning greater responsibility for their parenting roles.

Many absent fathers end up married and attending other churches as if nothing has changed. They placidly assume that they have little or no parenting obligations to their first offspring. After all, they now have a new family to take care of. Pastors can help to educate these absent fathers about their dual responsibilities.

Churches need to be more active in providing divorce counseling for parents and problem counseling for the children.

Competent, trained Christian counselors, both professional and laymen, are becoming more readily available to serve the church either on staff or by referral. It is important for the church to take advantage of these resources and to make them available to single parents. Divorce is always a painful situation for parents and especially for children. But it is my belief that many of the damaging consequences of divorce I have discussed throughout this book can be avoided through caring counseling. The Christian church, always the defender of the family, can be a means for doing this. The crisis confronting the family in our age needs courageous remedial action. If Christians don't take this action, who will?

CHAPTER 14

Building a Blended Family

As divorced persons remarry, they form an estimated thirteen hundred new stepfamilies *every day* in the United States. Unfortunately, almost 60 percent of these remarriages will end in yet another divorce.

There are many reasons why second or third marriages fail, but in my opinion one stands out above all others: The couple fails to successfully blend their two families.

The term *blended*, as I will use it here, means the merging of two single parents and their children into an effective, functioning, healthy, new nuclear family. Sometimes only one spouse brings children from a previous marriage. While the blending task would seem a little easier here, it is still a pretty difficult one.

As a general rule (and all general rules have their exceptions), it can be stated that the more children there are in a blending family, the greater will be the strain on that family. This follows simply because there are many more individuals whose needs will have to be taken into account. And since the joining of the two families can almost double the size of the family, a considerable readjustment will need to be made by everyone.

Living in a large original family is not the same as living in a large blended family. Large families can be a lot of fun. Children from large families are typically healthier and happier than those from small families. But they became large gradually. Large blended families are made instantly! And just like instant anything is not quite the same as the real thing, instant large families will test the character even of angels!

My focus in this chapter will not be on the stepparenting task so much as it will be on the more complex task of blending the family. This is a task that demands a serious commitment if it is going to be successful. If it turns out to be an impossible task, then the marriage must still survive. Whatever the outcome, you have to ensure that your primary relationship as husband and wife remains unbroken.

At the outset let me emphasize that there is not just one way to blend a family. There are many ways a family can learn to live together. If you have some ideal way in mind, then dump it right now! Successful blended families take many forms. I've known families to succeed where for years some of the children have never spoken to each other and where separate mealtimes had to be arranged just to keep the peace. If all is fair in love and war, then any strategy and model is fair game in blending a family.

The most crucial point around which success revolves is the love of the parents for each other that made them determined to survive. They grew strong and won out over personality differences and conflicts among their children by maintaining a strong commitment to each other.

What Do You Bring to Your New Family?

To understand the process of blending, you need to begin by inventorying what you bring to the new family. It helps to be honest here and to face up to the cold facts of reality.

Reviewing what you bring will also help you to anticipate where the pitfalls are and what problems may arise. With careful forethought you will be able to cut off trouble before it gets a foothold.

For instance, I recall working with one divorced mother whose eight-year-old son resented coming home from school to an empty apartment. Being somewhat immature for his age and suffering from a severe case of separation anxiety, the boy would mope around the apartment until his mother arrived home from work. Then for an hour or two afterward, he continued to be obstinate, negative, and difficult to handle.

Clearly, the boy just could not contain his anger at being left alone. Fortunately, the mother understood this and knew his anger would be a problem in her new marriage. Her intended husband had two older girls who went home with friends until their father collected them on his way home from work. I asked the mother how the son could be helped to overcome his anger and separation anxiety. As we reviewed the case together, the mother told me that her sister lived near enough for the son to go there after school. The sister had a son, just slightly older. The boy adored his older cousin. So at least for the first year of the new marriage, her son could stay with his cousin until his mother picked him up after work. She put it to the boy, and he jumped at the idea. An obvious problem had been foreseen and trouble avoided.

Taking an Inventory of Potential Problems

Here is an inventory that could suggest potential future problems for your new family:

1. Review old habits.

Ask yourself: What patterns of behavior, healthy or unhealthy, could cause problems? For instance, do your children tease each other excessively? Do they fight over personal territory? Are they easily irritated by each other? Your answers should flag areas that will need special attention.

2. Review old fears.

Ask yourself: What fears do my children have? Do the younger children fear the dark, the neighborhood, a bully at school, a teacher, or dogs? Dogs may be a problem if your new partner has a pet pit bull he intends to bring into the family!

3. Review patterns of past conflict.

Do your children balk at too much authority? Does your new spouse tend to be a bit of an authoritarian? Your children may view the children from the "other side" with great suspicion. Previous problems with authority figures may give rise to new problems.

4. Review conflicts between siblings.

Previous severe conflicts between siblings will worsen in the new family situation. A child from one side will try to turn others against the victim or may even form alliances with other children. These patterns must be identified ahead of time and dealt with. Get help if necessary, but don't carry old wars with you into a new family.

5. Review previous behavior problems.

If a child acts up, misbehaves at school, steals, tells lies, bullies, or cheats, don't expect these problems to go away without intentional intervention. The new family situation provides a whole new playing field for these inappropriate behaviors to flourish. Don't be blind to your own children's personalities and behavior problems.

6. Review previous emotional problems.

Children with emotional problems (such as severe anxiety or depressive tendencies) do not adjust well without help in a new family situation. Some emotional problems can be brought under control quickly with appropriate medication or therapy, and this will help the child by improving his or her copying ability. Don't hesitate, therefore, to get this help. It is surprising how often obvious severe depression or an overreactive hormonal system is overlooked as a cause for emotional misbehavior. Seek competent professional help before attempting to merge two families.

Obstacles to Building a Blended Family

What obstacles clearly get in the way of building a satisfactory merger between two families? Mostly, these inhibiting factors can be seen as "hangovers" of unresolved issues from a previous marriage.

Stella's story provides a good example of such a hangover. Her husband walked out on her when she was six months pregnant. He said he had fallen in love with Stella's closest friend. Abandoned by her husband both financially and emotionally and betrayed by her best friend, Stella became a recluse. She pulled away from her friends and family. She had the baby (a son) and set about building her life without benefit of any close friends for support.

She was so hurt by the betrayal and abandonment of her ex-husband that she came to distrust everyone. She feared that her friends would betray her, so she kept herself at a safe distance from all close relationships.

Six years passed. Then she met Frank, a divorced salesman, who came to work at the same company where Stella was employed. Frank swept her off her feet, and for a while Stella experienced trust and love again. They married and within the first week she began to doubt Frank's love. She became jealous, suspicious, distrustful, and, at times, even blatantly paranoid. She feared that Frank would abandon her as her first husband had.

Of course, all of this had an impact on her son. He became difficult to control. On several occasions he violently attacked Frank, wanting to protect his mother in his own childish way.

The new marriage was rapidly deteriorating when Frank realized that Stella's fears were quite understandably connected with an unresolved hurt from her previous marriage. He sought professional help, not just for Stella, but for the whole family. In just a few weeks of therapy, the relationships began to improve.

Sometimes the hangover concerns children. For instance, fears, anger, and behavior problems brought on by an alcoholic parent can seriously jeopardize attempts to build a blended family. Jealousy on the part of parents or children, unresolved resentment toward a previous spouse, and personality quirks will all need to be dealt with if you are going to maximize the healthiness of the new family.

I marvel at times just how true the Bible is. The sins of the fathers (and mothers) are passed on to the children "from generation to generation." The establishing of a new family is the ideal time to break the neurotic hereditary pattern and start the family game with new rules.

Trim Down Your Expectations

Not surprisingly, having very high expectations for how the new family will function can also be an obstacle.

It is natural that when you have been disappointed the first time around, you will have high expectations for future relationships. By all means set your goals high for building the best family relationship you can. But don't set your expectations unreasonably high, or you are bound to fail. You are better off being as realistic as possible. Face your obstacles courageously. Look at your problems openly. Expect that there will be some areas of conflict and misunderstanding and be prepared to deal with them. Plan to overcome them and always remember: Good marriages, as well as healthy families, are like beautiful gardens—they become beautiful because of the deliberate and painstaking care and attention given to them. Left to themselves, gardens degenerate to piles of weeds and trash.

Unrealistic expectations put too much pressure on all the members of a family. Usually the expectations are "borrowed" from some other idealized family or from fantasy. There is no single way for families to be. Some sit down and eat meals together. Others eat at different times and in different places. Some do things together, others go their separate ways. Both ways are acceptable.

It can almost certainly spell doom if you try to force a family to conform to some idealized pattern. Allow your family to find its own unique form of togetherness. This is the best guarantee of success.

In fact, the idea that each family is unique and needs to discover and affirm its own uniqueness can be both liberating and enhancing. I recall that as a boy of seven or eight (long before my parents divorced) I would look at other families and closely observe how they functioned. Their way always seemed right, and our way seemed wrong. They seemed to function as a unit. We seemed to be disorganized. They had to go in at a certain time after dark because their mother was very strict, and we sat around bored and alone after dark.

One day I opened up a conversation with my buddy from the "ideal" family. In my own way I told him about how I perceived them (I didn't even know the meaning of the word at the time). To my amazement he said that they all envied my freer lifestyle and easygoing parents. They enjoyed being in my home more than I did. I preferred to be in theirs. What confusion!

This discovery was an important one for me. It taught me that each family is unique. Value this uniqueness. Respect it. And above all, learn to be happy and content with this uniqueness. Perhaps if my parents had understood this principle a little better, their marriage would not have ended in divorce. But there I go—expecting too much again!

Building a New Identity As a Blended Family

Continuing on the theme of each family's uniqueness, let me say that nowhere is it more applicable than in the blended family. While a new identity must emerge for the new family, parents must be open enough to accept the fact that there are limitations on how far a blended family can be blended into a single entity. You may have to settle for several separate units.

I would go so far as to advise couples not even to try building a single entity. Focus rather on building an identity. This should allow for sufficient diversity to give everyone the freedom to become themselves. If the family feels fragmented to you, so be it! Let it find its own unique way of relating.

How one proceeds to build this uniqueness will depend largely on the age of the children. A mother with an infant who marries a man without any children and can have no further children herself is in a far better position to build a new family entity than two parents each with three children each, ranging in age from six to sixteen. In this latter case, the parents must allow for a far greater variation of what it means to be a nuclear family.

A helpful way to visualize your new blended family is to think of it as comprising two "mini-families." Each will have its own distinctive identities, patterns of behaving, and quirks. It will take time, perhaps as long as three to five years, for any significant blending to occur. Years may pass before the family develops a strong sense of identity.

It may never happen for some. But believe me, this is quite acceptable. The ultimate goal should not be to make everyone feel that they belong to one family, but rather to make everyone free to live together in Christian love, acceptance, and peaceful coexistence.

This is the only acceptable goal. Write it down on a card and keep it posted where you can read it regularly:

THE ONLY GOAL FOR MY FAMILY IS THAT
WE MAY LIVE TOGETHER IN CHRISTLIKE LOVE,
ACCEPTANCE, AND PEACEFUL COEXISTENCE.

If, in the process, an identity as a single family evolves, then treat this as icing on the cake—a little bonus you weren't expecting!

Stages in the Blending of a Family

There are some clearly identifiable stages in the blending of a family. Each stage, if understood, can be helped along by careful planning.

The first stage is to help each member accept each other. This takes time. Much will depend on the children's ages. Very young children and teenagers generally move quickly toward acceptance. Small children don't know better, and older teenagers have the social skills to make the adjustments necessary. It's the children in-between, from five to thirteen, who have the greatest difficulty. It can be helpful to point out the difference between accepting someone and liking someone. No one can be forced to like another person. Liking is an emotional attitude, and it only comes after you really know someone well. Acceptance is a matter of courtesy. It can be given in a moment. You just decide that someone else has as much right to be there as you do. It is a behavior, not a feeling, in which you do kind things and say gentle words. It shows respect for other people's property and person.

Present your expectation that there will be basic acceptance by all in a matter-of-fact way, at a family conference or even to each child individually. Praise each child for being courteous and showing respect for another. Set up clear consequences (for instance, taking a privilege away) for any behaviors not consistent with acceptance. Faithfully follow through on every stated consequence.

Above all, be patient and long-suffering yourself. Don't expect your children to do what you don't model to them.

The second stage is to set up a system of control. Here is where problems really begin to emerge. Couples make more mistakes here, I find, than in almost an other area of family life.

The establishment of an executive system within the family and the ability of each parent to set limits for and offer guidance to each child, is essential.

At the outset, let me distinguish clearly between punishment and discipline. Punishment is a "hurting back" for the hurts experienced by the parents. Discipline is a teaching activity, designed to help children learn appropriate behavior. Punishment is mostly harmful. Discipline is always helpful. The essential differences can be summarized as follows:

Punishment	Discipline
Always reacts in anger.	Always reacts with calmness.
Always seeks to retaliate.	Always seeks to help.
Seldom gives advance warning.	Always provides a warning.
Reacts out of impatience.	Is always patient.
Is motivated by revenge.	Is motivated by love.

Before you ever react to a child's behavior and to ensure that you are in a discipline mode and not a punishment mode, ask yourself the following questions:

1. Am I too angry to be objective and helpful?
2. Is my motive to hurt or help?
3. Did I give adequate warning so that the child had an opportunity to change or avoid the consequence?
4. Is there, even now, an opportunity for the child to change his or her behavior?

If your answer is yes to the first two questions and no to the second two, you are likely to be caught up in punishment rather than discipline.

The fundamental principles for effective discipline are simple:

1. Whenever your child does something you disapprove of, tell the child calmly not to do it again.

2. Set up a clear consequence at that time for any repetition of the undesired behavior. The consequence must match the behavior and be fair. Taking away TV watching for a month because Sally failed to tidy up her bedroom is excessive punishment. Discuss with your child what is a *fair* consequence. Also remember, children have short memories, so don't expect them to remember yesterday's threats. Remind them at the time of the behavior of your request and give them an opportunity to correct their mistake or restore omitted behavior.

3. Invoke the consequence, without fail, if the child refuses to comply. Provided the child understands what is desired and the consequence is fair, the result is always positive.

4. If the child refuses to comply, then increase the severity of the consequence. Always provide a way out so a child can correct the behavior and restore the privilege.

5. Always reserve physical discipline for dangerous behaviors. "The next time you throw sand in your sister's face . . . ," or "The next time you run into the street . . . ," can be followed by, "I will spank you." And then make sure you are not angry when you spank.

It is preferred that the natural parent of the child do all disciplining, for reasons I will explain in the next section.

The third stage in the blending of a new family is one of harmonious functioning. Perhaps I should say "relative harmony." It is unreasonable to expect that total harmony will ever emerge. A fair degree of mutual respect and affection is always possible, however.

Who Should Do the Disciplining?

A serious error made by many stepparents is that they take on too much responsibility for disciplining the other children. An important principle to remember is: *Each natural parent should take primary responsibility for disciplining his or her own children.*

Why do I say this? Very simply, because if you don't, you violate the child's sense of justice. Deep down, children accept that the right to discipline belongs to the natural parent. They resent it when that right is exercised by a stepparent, no matter how justified the discipline.

It's just a fact of human behavior. Many stepparents become very upset about this. They can see all the flaws in the stepchild (they often don't see the same faults in their own children) and believe they know exactly how to deal with the brat. Their very attitude disqualifies them from being fair. Some mothers gladly surrender responsibility for discipline to the new partner without realizing just how much resentment this causes.

I know there are exceptions, but they are few and far between. Severe and dangerous behaviors must be dealt with, and it really doesn't matter who does the disciplining here. Get the police to do it, if necessary. But everyday problems of conflict and adjustment are best handled by the natural parent and should include the absent natural parent whenever possible. As a stepparent, you may finally earn the right and respect to be the one who disciplines, but at the beginning play it safe, support your spouse, and take a back seat.

Resolving Conflicts

Every parent should have good conflict-resolution skills. Conflicts arise every day with amazing regularity in every family. Families with no conflicts are unnatural! I happen to believe that freedom from conflict only comes about much later in life after your children have left the nest. An absence of overt conflict may not necessarily be a good sign. It may only be a thin crust over a boiling volcano.

Family members each have their own needs, and these will inevitably clash with the needs of others. In a blending family, a whole new set of needs are dumped into the center of the game. Healthy families are healthy because they know how to resolve their conflicts quickly, and parents who are skilled in conflict resolution make better parents!

There are four basic types of family conflict:

1. Personality conflicts.

These are the most common. Simply put, two people just don't like each other. Sometimes it is because they are so much alike, and each detests what they see about themselves in the other. At other times, conflict may occur because the two are opposites, and one can't understand the other. They clash all the time. The one says cold, the other replies hot. One says east, the other west. They always seem to be at the opposite ends of every issue.

Such conflicts are really not a problem if the parties can just behave in a civil manner toward each other. Demand that respect be shown at all times.

Extreme personality conflicts may require that you totally separate the children. Put them in separate bedrooms. Let them use separate closets, bathrooms, clothes, and even mealtimes. It is a great mistake to force people to live in close proximity to each other if they clash severely.

2. Conflicts over personal needs.

Here a child may have a strong need that cannot be met, and it surfaces as anger or resentment. For example, a young boy separated from his natural father and needing his affection and attention may become overly aggressive and even destructive. Or a daughter needing Mom's attention may cry a lot because Mother is spending so much time with her new spouse.

The solution here is simple: Help your children meet their needs, and if this is not possible, then give them ample opportunity to talk about why they have this need. Often children are not aware of why they are in conflict. Sensitive and patient listening will help both you and your child discover the source of the conflict. Once you know its source, a solution will clearly present itself.

3. Misunderstanding conflicts.

Accept the fact that there will be many moments when your children (natural and step) will hate you. Hate is simply thwarted love.

Sometimes a child is too immature to understand. As parents we don't take time to explain or give reasons why things are the way they are. Parents owe their children clear explanations and an opportunity to work through any misunderstanding.

4. Authority conflicts.

Parents owe their children a measure of authority. This provides security and a clear message about the boundaries of freedom. Families that are dominated by "child power" are characterized by chaos and unhappiness. Unfortunately, if parents do not assert authority when children are very young, it will be very difficult to begin to do it when they are older.

Don't be unreasonable, and avoid being physical. Learn to say no and say it often without feeling guilty. Say it with firmness and consistency. Children should be corrected and disciplined as often as necessary, since this is how they learn. Never, however, use labels like bad, evil, no good, or stupid. These undermine a child's sense of personal worth, and no one deserves to be treated this way, least of all a child.

Some Principles of Conflict Resolution

The topic of conflict resolution is too big to deal with here. There are three important goals to keep in mind, however, whenever you try to resolve conflicts between children or between a child and a parent:

1. **Everyone must win.** No conflict resolution is effective if someone loses.

2. **Try hard to get understanding.** Understanding is more important than agreement.

3. **Never take away a person's self-respect.** No conflict resolution is effective that solves problems at the expense of someone's self-respect.

How can these goals be accomplished? By first trying to understand each side's point of view. Showing that you understand is more important than reaching an agreement.

Each of these goals has an important function in mind. No one likes to be a loser. Small children do not have the capacity to accept failure without losing face, so whenever there is a conflict, each party to the conflict should come out feeling they haven't lost their sense of value.

The art of working out compromises is very helpful here. Ask yourself, "What can I trade to get the other side to give up what they want?"

If, for example, two children are bickering over whether to go to a movie or go bowling, neither need lose. If it is a movie tonight, then it can be bowling next week, or vice versa. It is amazing how easy it is to find a compromise or trade-off for most conflicts, so that both parties win.

Understanding another person is more important than agreeing with the other person. Most of us feel a strange tension, however, when we try to understand an opposing position. We fear we may have to change! And this is precisely the value of focusing on coming to understand rather than on reaching agreement. You might just change your mind!

Let me illustrate. Suppose your teenage stepson wants to spend a weekend away at his buddy's home. You dislike his friend and distrust his morals. You would prefer that your stepson go to church on Sunday with the rest of the family. Finally you exercise your authority and say no. You explain that you don't like the friend's morals. Your stepson says, "He's a nice guy." You say, "He's a bum." You would prefer him to change his friend, but he prefers the one he has.

What do you do? Focus on getting understanding first. Forget about whether you can get him to agree with your opinion of his friend. In fact, you will probably never get him to agree with you. So, sit down and talk. Say, "I know we don't agree about your friend, but I do want to understand about him. Tell me about him." Stick with trying to understand. Even if nothing else changes, your stepson will respect you more for trying to understand his point of view. And there is always the chance that you or he may change your positions.

Whatever transpires in your attempt to resolve conflicts, protect your spouse's or child's self-respect. This is an obligation all parents have at all times. Self-esteem is the cornerstone of good mental health. A child who is continually criticized and devalued, or is made to feel inadequate or always wrong, who is constantly being compared with more competent siblings, cousins, or peers, will never try to improve. In fact, these children become unmotivated, lazy, and rebellious. Children have an uncanny way of "living down to your expectations."

Here Are Some Important Don'ts

Don't let children run the show. Often, especially when divorced parents are overrun with guilt, too much priority is given to the needs of children. Parents become too afraid to say no, give orders, or to discipline. They fear loss of love and want to avoid confrontation. Don't abdicate your responsibility. Show me a family run by children, and I will show you cowardly parents trying to buy love.

Don't be afraid to be boss. By nature, children test limits to see how much they can get away with. It's instinctive! And they don't respect parents who give in. Rules should be clearly stated and enforced.

Don't expect to have love feelings for your stepchildren at the outset. Don't expect your stepchildren to show love to you either. Love is something that must be earned. You give love first, and you will someday be rewarded by having it returned.

Don't compare your stepchildren to your own children. This only heightens conflict within the family.

Don't play favorites with any of the children. Be fair to all.

Here Are Some Important Do's

Do respond with loving behavior regardless of what a child does to you. Consistency is important.

Do talk to your children regularly to find out what they're thinking and feeling. Regular family conferences can help to reduce misunderstandings.

Do allow all feelings to be expressed and talked about. To suppress feelings is to store up trouble. However, do not allow feelings, especially anger, to be acted out. It is sufficient just to talk about them.

Do be open to learning from the new personalities of your stepchildren.

Do spend a lot of time in prayer. Ask God to keep your love fresh and alive for your new spouse, for your children, and for God's gift to you—your stepchildren. See your task of parenting and befriending them as a special calling. Forge a godly family with the same determination you would use to serve on any mission field. No task is more holy than this!

Study Guide

Read each chapter through at least once before working through this study guide. Read it again as you respond to these questions.

Chapter 1 ✦ Divorced at Twelve

1. Without condoning divorce, make a list of some of the reasons why couples finally seek marital separation. Which of these reasons do you see as legitimate? Which are not?

2. How does being a Christian change any of these reasons for seeking divorce? How does it not change them?

3. If you are a child of divorce (or know someone who is), what emotional aftereffects can you identify in your life?

4. What factors, experiences, or persons helped bring healing to your emotions? How can you be helpful to others who now need this healing?

Chapter 2 ✦ The Damaging Effects of Divorce

1. What are the dangers inherent in believing that divorce has no damaging effects on children?

(201)

2. The damaging effects of divorce on children depend largely on the stage of childhood when the divorce takes place. At what stages would a child be minimally affected, and at what stage the most? Why?

3. Why are some divorces more damaging in their effects on children than others?

4. There are some circumstances where divorce, or at least separation, might be the best course of action. What are these circumstances?

5. Examine again the painful feelings explored in the second part of this chapter. Note the progression from one to the next. How can each of these feelings be reduced or transformed to positive and healing feelings?

Chapter 3 ◆ Healing Your Resentment

1. Where must all healing begin? What implications does this have for your life?

2. Why do you think resentment is such a destructive emotion?

3. We cling to, justify, and accumulate resentments like no other of God's creations. How does this relate to our sinful and selfish natures?

4. Review again the steps on how to deal with resentments, applying them to your own life-circumstances.

Chapter 4 ◆ Common Mistakes Made by Divorced Parents

1. How do you usually try to deal with your guilt feelings? What provision did God make for all our guiltiness?

2. Most absent parents are fathers. While many children survive quite adequately without a father in the home, what does a father bring to a child's development?

3. Why is it easier for a child to adjust to the changes that divorce brings if these changes occur slowly? Are there circumstances when sudden and total change is preferable?

4. We grow stronger and become more like the people God wants us to be when we learn from past mistakes. Make a short list of mistakes you have made in your life. What have you learned from them?

Chapter 5 ✦ Your Child's Feelings

1. A child's feeling world is very precious—and very vulnerable. How can we safeguard these feelings before, during, and after a divorce?

2. Of all the feelings a child can experience in a breakup of the home, which would you identify with the most? Why?

3. The feelings a child experiences in divorce parallel those seen in all grieving. In what ways is divorce like death? What dies? What lives on?

4. Examine the painful feelings explored in the second part of this chapter. Note the progression from one to the next. How can each of these feelings be reduced or transformed to positive and healing-producing feelings?

Chapter 6 ✦ What Children Learn from Divorce

1. Divorce is a learning experience—for good or bad. What does conflict teach children?

2. Why are positive and healthy behaviors and reactions more difficult to model for children than destructive ones?

3. The six resiliency-building suggestions given in this chapter can help all children, not just those going through divorce. Select one of these suggestions and list practical ways you can implement it with your children.

4. Do you have difficulty being honest with your children? Why?

Chapter 7 ◆ Anxiety and the Divorced Child

1. Why are children prone to anxiety and what is it about marital breakup that threatens a child's security?

2. How much do you fear rejection? Can you trace the origin of this fear to early life experiences?

3. Review the three categories of anxiety symptoms. Which is the most difficult to cope with for you?

4. Why is it so important for a parent to understand what a child is feeling? Does it influence how the child adjusts to divorce?

Chapter 8 ◆ Anger and the Divorced Child

1. A child's anger does not always show itself directly. In what other ways can it reveal itself?

2. What do we mean when we say anger is passive? Can you recognize your passive anger behaviors?

3. Our culture is terribly confused about the appropriateness of anger Review the differences between the feeling of anger

and the behavior of anger. Which is appropriate for the Christian?

4. Men and boys generally have one thing in common when it comes to emotions? What is it, and how can we help them overcome it?

Chapter 9 ◆ Improving Your Child's Self-Esteem

1. What can damage the development of a child's self-esteem?

2. How is self-love different from self-esteem, and how is high self-esteem different from conceit?

3. What mistakes have you made in building your child's self-esteem? What can you do to rectify this situation?

4. Of all the ways divorce can damage a child's self-esteem, which do you think (or which have you experienced) is the most damaging?

Chapter 10 ◆ Depression and the Divorced Child

1. Why does divorce cause depression in children? Are there ways this can be avoided?

2. What is the purpose of this depression?

3. When you suffer a loss, can you recognize the signs of depression in yourself? Which is the most prominent sign?

4. We develop perspective on our losses best when we talk about them, but often children don't have the skills to talk about their feelings. What other ways can be used to help children express their feelings?

Chapter 11 ◆ Your Ex-Spouse Is Still a Parent

1. Why does one parent in divorce usually want to completely cut off the other from the children?

2. What barriers commonly make it difficult for the absent parent to build a good relationship with children left behind?

3. How can these barriers be reduced?

4. What factors would make an ex-spouse unsuitable as a parent?

Chapter 12 ◆ Becoming a Stepparent

1. Stepparenting is never easy. From a child's perspective, what fantasies are upset by remarriage?

2. Place yourself in a child's position. How would you feel about your parent's remarriage?

3. What advice would you give your parents on how to go about remarriage?

Chapter 13 ◆ Becoming an Effective Single Parent

1. Why is single parenting more arduous than parenting as a couple?

2. Discuss the benefits and disadvantages of single parenting.

3. The workplace interaction with the family is more hazardous for the mother than for the father. What should mothers do to minimize this interaction?

4. Single fathers (as well as married fathers for that matter) need to open up the emotional expressiveness of their deeper personality. What are some of the ways a father can do this?

5. Discuss some of the ways the church can help single parents to be more effective?

Chapter 14 ◆ Building a Blended Family

1. What does one bring from a previous marriage to a blended family? Why is it important to be aware of this carryover?

2. What obstacles are there to effectively building a blended family? What can be done to overcome these obstacles?

3. What goals do you want to set for your new family? Are they attainable?

4. What conflicts are you experiencing at this stage of your life? What plans can you make to overcome them?

Dr. Archibald D. Hart is professor of psychology and former dean of the Graduate School of Psychology at Fuller Theological Seminary in Pasadena, California. Originally from South Africa, Dr. Hart is the respected author of eighteen books, including *Stress and Your Child, Overcoming Anxiety, The Hidden Link Between Adrenaline and Stress,* and *The Sexual Man.* He is a highly acclaimed lecturer who has traveled internationally as well as throughout the United States. He and his wife, Kathleen, have three grown daughters and seven grandchildren. They reside in Arcadia, California.